I Break for Butterflies

A Simple Guide to Spiritual Awakening

Dr. Barbie J. Taylor

SQUARE CIRCLES
PUBLISHING

I BRAKE FOR BUTTERFLIES
A Simple Guide to Spiritual Awakening
by Dr. Barbie J. Taylor

Copyright © 2017 Dr. Barbie J. Taylor

All rights reserved.
No part of this publication may be reproduced, stored in a retrievalsystem or transmitted in any form or by any means, electronic, mechanical, photocopying, recording or otherwise, without prior permission in writing of the publisher.

Cover and interior: Syrp & Co.
Front cover butterfly image: shutterstock.com
Front over road image: wallpaperstock.net
Back cover photo: Brenda Klinger

ISBN: 978-0-9982556-2-0

Published by Square Circles Publishing
www.SquareCirclesPublishing.com
PO Box 9682
Pahrump, NV 89060

This book is dedicated to Mother Teresa
who personally blessed me when
I was in India in 1985

Photo by the author

Contents

	Publisher's Page	ii
	Dedication	iii
	Acknowledgments	vii
	Foreword by Brad Steiger	ix
1	Butterflies Are Free	1
2	To Be or Not to Be Happy	11
3	Spirit Is	18
4	We Are Not Alone	31
5	The Visitors	43
6	Honoring All Life	56
7	Changes…Changes…Changes	62
8	Lessons Happen	67
9	Learning to Let Go	72
10	Coming Together	75
11	Playful Passion	80
12	Kids, Parents, and Other Strangers	87
13	Jobs Are Optional	94
14	Death Is Not a Requirement	103
	Resources	113
	About the Author	123

Acknowledgments

As with most literary projects, this one has been a team effort. I want to thank Lori Evans for typing several drafts of the initial manuscript, and Faye Frost who offered invaluable assistance in editing the original draft. I thank Brad Steiger for the Foreword and the benefit of his considerable literary experience. For moral support I have to acknowledge the "Sunday Night Potluck" contingent and Don Campbell who spurred me on with the original draft. I greatly appreciate, as well, the artwork by Beth Campbell for the chakra diagram.

My undying gratitude goes always to my son, Steve Taylor, my daughter, Tamalyn Taylor, and my deceased parents, Eileen Merrill and Dr. Clarence S. Merrill, who cheer me on in spirit.

Thanks to Saskia Raevouri of Square Circles Publishing for revising and publishing this new edition of my book.

I also want to acknowledge Richard Bach, author of *Illusions, Jonathan Livingston Seagull,* and other successful books, who unbeknownst to him, first inspired me as a writer. Most of all, though, I am grateful to "Spirit" for teaching me throughout life to always choose love.

Foreword by Brad Steiger

IN THIS TIMELY and comforting book, *I Brake for Butterflies,* Dr. Barbie J. Taylor repeatedly assures us that even in these turbulent times of troubled transitions and societal and cultural transformations, we still have choices.

I think this book will especially appeal to young people, who in their collective dismay over the increasing amounts of negativity bombarding them from the world that they have inherited, are apt to consider their personal decisions to be of little consequence in the general malaise that affects the *zeitgeist* of our nation. "Dr. Barbie" confidently assures all of us—young and old—that hope has not gone out of style and that there are still numerous opportunities that will permit us to embrace happiness and love.

It is also comforting to know that she does not pretend to lecture us from the safe and secure Olympian distance of the self-proclaimed Master Teacher, "Dr. Barbie" freely admits that she, too, is still seeking and searching and that she, too, is far from perfect.

A dear mentor of mine told me long ago that life is a "Do-It-Yourself-Kit." "Dr. Barbie" appears to acknowledge this assertion as one of the eternal verities. We can be guided by others and from time to time we can accept their advice, but the final and actual "doing" is truly up to us as individuals.

Readers of this book will be fortunate, indeed, to have one such as Dr. Barbie Taylor as their guide and their advisor. Although she gives marvelous counsel urging us to move into the light, rather than to recede into the darkness, she is quick to remind us that the final choice will always be ours.

She does, however, add a note of her own wishful thinking that from the myriad choices before us—from delectable, delicious, and delightful to dreary, dreadful, and deadly—we decide to choose love and happiness and resolve to set out to change the world as we know it.

I will add to "Dr. Barbie's" hope for unconditional love the weight of my own wish—that each reader shall make such a positive decision. And I am confident that after one reads this marvelous little book, it shall be so.

Brad Steiger
Forest City, Iowa

1

Butterflies Are Free

I was suddenly thrown forward in the car as my husband slammed on the brakes. We were driving through our neighborhood of turn-of-the-century homes and picket fences in Morgantown, West Virginia. I had been looking for something on the floor and was looking down, so the sudden jolt against my seatbelt was unexpected.

In a playful but apologetic manner, Nand said, "I'm sorry, but I brake for birds."

I laughed and said, "That's okay. I understand because I do it, too. In fact, I brake for butterflies!" I was remembering the drive through the countryside the previous day when I had suddenly hit my brakes as a lovely, large butterfly fluttered across the road.

As soon as the words came out of my mouth, I realized that braking for butterflies was a metaphor for my philosophy of life. I have always had a reverence for life. If I find a cricket or spider in my house, I place a glass over it then slide a postcard under the opening of the glass, so I can carry it to safety outside. With a butterfly, I feel an even closer connection because it is a thing of beauty that to me represents freedom and transformation. It enters life as a caterpillar and must go into the dark silence of the cocoon before emerging as a beautiful, winged creature that soars into the light of day. What a perfect symbol for spiritual transformation.

The event took place long ago, seemingly in another lifetime. Nand and I divorced in 1989, after a twelve-year relationship. He chose to stay in the East, while I returned to the West. It hasn't always been easy since then, and I've sometimes wondered about my penchant for change throughout my life. Will I always be a wanderer? Once I actually looked up the meaning of my given name, Barbara, and it said, "wanderer, stranger, or alien." I have certainly felt "alien" at times in this third-dimensional reality, but I have also lived a life of great adventure and magic.

I want to begin this book by sharing a personal story with you about the type of universal magic I'm talking about. It's not the magic of magicians, but rather the miraculous events we co-create with the divine forces of the universe. These are not random events. They're something we create or tap into because of our consciousness—our attitudes, beliefs, and willingness to choose the path of love over fear. The fact that we are constantly making choices is a significant and absolutely necessary lesson to learn, if we are going to take control of our lives in a positive way.

My favorite story of universal magic happened to me in 1985, while I was traveling in India for six-and-a-half weeks. The way the trip evolved in the first place was pretty unusual. In 1978, when I was finishing up my psychology internship at the Long Beach VA Hospital, a friend of mine introduced me to an Indian holy man by the name of Sai Baba who is now deceased. Not only did I read the book, *Sai Baba, Man of Miracles,* I also drove to the Sai Baba Center in Hollywood to pick up some more books about this unusual man on the other side of the world. I found it fascinating that a man born in a tiny, obscure village in southern India, who had not traveled abroad to any great extent, who still lived in this small village, could attract a following of millions from all over the world.

The book described in detail the many documented miracles Sai Baba had performed and his openness to all spiritual paths. As a child, I had loved the stories in the Bible about the miracles performed by Jesus, especially when he said that one day you, too, would be able to do this and more. Here was a man doing exactly what Jesus had said, performing miracles like in the Bible (John 14:12).

The book about Sai Baba said he might be less available to his followers after the age of sixty, so I decided then and there I wanted to go to India before that time to pay my respects to this holy man who had done so much for so many people. It was that intention, that thought, which set into motion my great adventure seven years later. In 1985, I was asked if I wanted to present a paper at the "Seventh International Congress of Sexology" that was meeting in New Delhi. At the time, I was busy building my private practice in Morgantown, West Virginia, so

I just laughed and declined the invitation, not taking it seriously at first. I couldn't imagine taking off on such a long and expensive trip, especially since I knew my husband would have no interest in traveling to India.

Several days later, I remembered my original desire to visit Sai Baba and realized this was an opportunity to fulfill that desire. I accepted the invitation with the realization I had nearly a year to put it all together. It just seemed like the right thing to do, and even Nand wasn't too shocked when I announced my plans. It would also put me in India immediately prior to Sai Baba's 60th birthday.

I found a small group of people who were going to India prior to my conference. They planned on visiting the holy sites then would conclude their trip at Sai Baba's ashram (a place where a holy person resides). The timing was perfect because it coincided with his birthday celebration, which was quite an event, to say the least. When we were there he married 600 village couples, gave their families a feast, put them all up at the ashram, and gave them wedding gifts of necessary household items and clothing for the wedding. This was just one of the planned special events for his birthday.

I spent nine days at the ashram, but the real "magic" began once I left there on my own to go to the New Delhi conference. After spending four weeks getting to know the country with others, I felt comfortable striking out on my own for the next three weeks.

On the plane to New Delhi, I sat next to a woman who turned out to be a classical dancer and fine artist from New Delhi. Her home was near the small hotel where I was staying, so she offered to drive me to my hotel from the airport. We had enjoyed our conversation, and she invited me to afternoon tea with her a few days later. She came and picked me up on the appointed afternoon, and we went over to her house, which was part of a government-owned complex because her husband was a diplomat. I never did meet him because he was somewhere on a diplomatic mission, but I did briefly meet her neighbor who came by to tell her about a trip to the doctor that afternoon. The doctor had diagnosed an intestinal problem I knew was associated with stress, so I suggested she might try hypnosis as a means of relaxing.

We had a brief conversation at that time and we discovered a connection with Morgantown. Her daughter-in-law had served her medical internship at the West Virginia School of Medicine in my hometown. It seemed incredible that I had traveled halfway around the world and ended up meeting this woman who knew Morgantown.

The neighbor left after our brief but interesting conversation. About five minutes later, her husband came over to talk with me. He asked if I would be willing to do some hypnosis sessions with his wife during my stay in New Delhi. My conference didn't start for another week, and I had no other plans. We agreed that I would work with her over that time, and they would become my tour guides. The names of my new-found host family were Vivek and Annu Nehru. They had an eighteen-year-old daughter, Ritu. They also had a driver who doubled as a security guard. He would accompany Ritu and me when we went anywhere together.

I had been reading in the New Delhi English newspaper about the memorial service being planned for Indira Gandhi, the former prime minister. She had been tragically assassinated the previous year by one of her own security guards in the garden of her residence. I wondered if there would be a place for foreigners at the memorial service, and imagined it taking place in some large auditorium. I asked Vivek if he thought there might be a way for me to attend the memorial. He considered it for a moment, then he said he would take care of it. I was glad to know that I would be able to go, given that I was in town during such an important event.

On the day of the memorial service, the Nehrus' driver picked me up at my hotel. Vivek and Ritu were in the car, but Annu had decided to stay home because she wasn't feeling well. I expected we would go to some large, public building. Instead, we drove into a nice residential area, dropped off the car, and went through a small gate into a large backyard area. I was surprised by the number of security personnel with automatic weapons. They were everywhere, and I saw at least three different types of military uniforms. Right beyond the gate was a metal detector we all went through in single file. This was certainly different from the public memorial I had expected to attend.

We were ushered into an area with beautiful carpets spread out over an expansive lawn. There was a small stage at the front. We were directed to sit right up front by the stage, as more Indian people continued to arrive, mostly couples and a few individual men. After everyone was seated on the carpeted area, there was a flurry of activity among the security guards.

Ritu leaned over to me and said, "Here comes the prime minister and his family."

Her statement was the first clue I had about what was going on. We were in the garden where Mrs. Gandhi had actually been shot, and it was the backyard of the private residence where the prime minister and his family lived. We were attending a service for just the family and heads of state. There I was, the only blue-eyed blonde in the place, and I was sitting right with the prime minister's family. He and his lovely wife plus their two young teenage children were no more than eight feet from me. It turned out that Vivek was the prime minister's uncle. Rajiv Gandhi had become the prime minister when his mother was murdered. Sadly, he was also assassinated in 1991, in a bombing attack, in spite of his ever-present heavy security. That family had been very much like the Kennedy family here in America.

The memorial service consisted of sitar music and poetry. Once everyone got settled, it lasted for about an hour, which was a long time for me to sit crossed-legged on the ground while squeezed between other family members. I had to shift my weight a few times, but I managed to remain poised. There was a whole bank of reporters on the other side of the stage, and photographers snapping pictures. The next day, Ritu and I were given a private tour of the president's palace by his secretary, a very proper gentleman in a military uniform. Vivek had made all the arrangements for us ahead of time.

When the "Seventh International Congress of Sexology" finally got underway about a week later, I gave several presentations, both individually and as part of two panel discussions. It was attended by a large, international crowd of sex educators, researchers and therapists. I was being interviewed by a reporter after one of my talks, and I just happened to mention that I had attended the private memorial service for Indira Gandhi. His eyes widened, and with obvious excitement in his voice he asked me, "Were you sitting with the family?" I told him I was, and he said, "All the reporters were trying to figure out who the blonde woman was who was sitting with the family."

Unbeknownst to me, I had apparently caused quite a stir with the media. I just wish I had checked the papers the next day. I may have found my picture on the front page. The reason I love this story so much is because it's the example from my own life that best reflects special, universal blessings. I went to New Delhi knowing no one, but within a three-week period I had sat with the prime minister and his family right in their backyard. I had attended a very special memorial service, and had a private tour of the presidential palace.

I also made some wonderful friends. It would be like a foreign doctor visiting the United States for the first time, and ending up at a private White House gathering—just by chance. I felt blessed and grateful for my special experiences, and I often wondered if on some other level of reality Sai Baba "arranged" all this for me as a special treat. That is impossible to prove, but the likelihood of it all happening by chance seems unlikely, too.

There have been many other times in my life when unusual things happened that were obviously not random events. I call them "cosmic coincidences," even though I know there is no such thing as a coincidence that is not in some way associated with consciousness.

In 1995, I decided to open my own office once again after working as a therapist for several years in other people's offices. I had been working for others since leaving my private practice back east in 1989, except for a brief time in Sedona, Arizona, in 1990. I wanted more time to work on this book and more freedom in my life. It was once again time for me to go back into private practice, but I had no idea how it was going to come together financially. In spite of that, I just *knew* it was time to do it. I gave my boss four weeks' notice, found a small new office, and started the ball rolling. I knew there would be several months delay between the first billing and the checks actually coming in. I was essentially walking away from my regular paychecks and taking a great leap of faith.

One day about a week into this process, I was doing my usual three-mile daily walk while carrying on an internal dialogue that went something like this: "It would be a whole lot easier to do all this if I had $10,000.

The next day a client asked me how my move was going. I told him that $10,000 would make it easier. That night when I got home, there was a telephone message from Judy, my youngest sister. The message asked me to give her a call and said it was about our elderly Aunt Dorothy. Judy lives in another state, and we usually communicate on birthdays, holidays, and a few other times during the year, so this was a rather unusual message.

I immediately gave Judy a call. She informed me that Dorothy was okay, but that she had been handling Dorothy's financial affairs because her memory was failing. I knew I would one day be one of the heirs to my aunt's estate, and I knew she had a certain amount of money because she had never spent any of it, and she had worked her whole life. Judy told me that Aunt Dorothy's estate had grown to the point that any more income from her various investments would only go to taxes, so Judy had suggested that my aunt give the one-time allowable tax-free gift to her heirs before she died.

So, Judy told me, "I'm sending you a check for $10,000 next week."

As one might expect, I was overjoyed by this much-needed financial windfall, but the fact that it was the exact amount I had wished for made it even more uncanny. That $10,000 gave me the freedom to practice on my own once again. It confirmed to me that I made the right decision at the right time. In fact, I believe I am in the right place, at the right time, doing the right thing. This belief has worked very well for me, but I am also fully aware that I create my own reality through my level of consciousness. It is not just *luck*. I also know that I can teach others to become consciously aware of their own creations in life. It is this consciousness that allows us to take charge of our lives and awaken to the spirit within each one of us. It is this transformation that is also so perfectly symbolized by the butterfly.

This book is about that spiritual process in every aspect of our lives, and it begins with the very basic understanding that we can choose to be fully conscious and fully aware—every thought and every action is essentially a choice. The first step is to decide to be a happy person in spite of the negativity that exists in the world, and that is where we will begin.

2

To Be or Not to Be Happy

Let's begin with the basics—learning to be happy. We are constantly making choices in our lives, but sometimes it doesn't feel that way. Most people act as though they are subject to random events, floating through life with little or no awareness of their own power, feeling helpless to alter or control their own lives. This is an illusion. Each of us is a powerful spiritual being. It's as though we carry with us a magical device with all the knowledge we will ever need, but no one told us how to turn the darn thing on. It's time to learn.

The magical device we all carry around with us is our own higher minds. The western educational system is geared toward teaching lots of facts, but we are not taught about how to use our minds. We are not taught that what we think and how we think has a direct relationship to how we experience our lives. This is the key to understanding that life is all about "choices." We can learn to use our minds to work for us, instead of against us.

Most of us have had the experience of being around people who always seem to be in a good mood or other people who seem crabby most of the time. Frequently, we refer to this as having "good vibes" or "bad vibes." This is actually more accurate than many people realize, because it is all about vibrations. When we learn to think in a positive way, it increases our vibrations or frequency; and thinking in a negative manner, decreases them. To play the game of life correctly, you must learn how to be happy by changing the way you think. That's how to *win* the game.

We need to recognize that thinking is only a habit. We have been taught to think in specific ways through our upbringing, our education, and our life experiences. Anything we have learned, we can unlearn or relearn. It's just a matter of creating a new habit—a new habit of thought, which isn't as difficult as you might imagine. However, it does take some practice and a little time and effort. No big deal, we are all eternal beings, anyway.

In order to change the way you are presently thinking, you must first become aware of *what* you are thinking. Begin to notice whether you are more often thinking positive things or negative things. It's especially important to notice what you were thinking immediately prior to an emotional response, although you may not have noticed before that thoughts precede feelings. Even if you are having an emotional reaction in response to some particular event, there is a mental interpretation of that event which comes first. Sometimes, that mental interpretation is at an unconscious level based on conditioning from your past; but for now, let's just keep it simple. The goal is to learn to have positive interpretations.

These mental interpretations are completely tied to your belief system. If you had the belief that out of every experience some good would come, your emotional responses would change dramatically. Even if what happened seemed negative to you. Choosing to recognize that you can learn a lesson from the experience can turn it into a positive. So you need to become aware not only of your thoughts, but also of your beliefs, and you need to create some new, more positive beliefs because your beliefs are also a choice.

When I was still in graduate school at the University of Washington, I became aware of the fact that beliefs have a major influence on what happens in our lives. If we always expect something negative to happen, we interpret experiences in such a way to prove ourselves to be correct. In other words, we will always find evidence to support our beliefs whether they are functional or dysfunctional. As a result, I decided to systematically change my beliefs to create a more positive existence. You can do it, too.

Begin to examine these beliefs more carefully, more rationally. You might say, "Kathy is fatter than I am, and she seems to be happy. What if I never lose weight—does that mean I can never be happy? The reality is there will always be people thinner than me, and there will always be people fatter than me. Maybe I can be happy, and it has nothing to do with my weight. In fact, I now choose to believe that I can be happy just as I am." You will actually lose weight more effectively by changing your belief, because a happier person is more successful than a person who continues to self-destruct to prove how unworthy they are.

Now, suppose your issue is money instead of weight. You might say, "There are a lot of rich people who don't seem to be very happy. Look at some of the movie stars and rock stars who just use their money to destroy themselves with drugs. Harry doesn't have much money, and he seems to be a pretty happy guy. Maybe happiness is not really linked to money. In fact, I know I can become happy whether or not I am ever financially independent."

This is a step in the right direction—choosing happiness and deleting old, dysfunctional beliefs. When you notice a tendency to fall into old habits of negative thinking, there is a wonderful technique that can help you turn it around called "thought stopping." As soon as you notice a negative thought or belief showing up in your mind, immediately picture a large, red stop sign, and say the word "stop" to yourself or out loud. You can even strengthen the effect of this technique by placing a rubber band on your wrist and snapping it each time you say "stop." It may seem silly, but this is a highly effective technique for making changes in your behavior. You are now systematically reconditioning yourself to change your thinking.

Once you start noticing the patterns of your beliefs and thoughts, you need to replace the negative with something positive. That's where affirmations come in. Essentially, an affirmation is just a positive statement, but the way you word it is important. The most powerful way to do this is to use the words, "I am," followed by whatever you want to say. For example, "I am now choosing to think in a positive way." Some people like to include their name to make it even more personal, such as, "I, Barbie, am now totally and completely happy."

Don't get caught up in whether or not it's a true statement. The idea is to make a statement that represents your ideal—this is what you want to create. You are reinforcing this new quality within your mind (which is where everything has to start) because it represents the positive change in your life. Whatever you focus on, especially if you use visual imagery, affirmations, and feelings, is what you eventually manifest in your life. That is why setting goals is so important.

However, just because you start saying, "I am a millionaire—I am a millionaire—I am a millionaire," does not mean you are going to wake up wealthy the next morning; but you are at least taking a step in the right direction, assuming that's what you want to create in your life.

What most people don't take into consideration when they are first learning about the power of the mind is that they may have significant blocks from this life or a previous life that get in the way of receiving. If you aren't a good receiver, it's very difficult, if not impossible, for God, Jesus, the universe, your guides or guardian angels (pick the term you prefer) to bless you. If a part of you keeps insisting that you are unworthy, guess what, you're not going to be able to manifest a lot of good stuff in your life.

So how do you get the internal cobwebs cleared out of your mind so you can attract good into your life? You've got to work on your hang-ups and learn to make changes in your attitude and perception of reality. This includes your thoughts and beliefs, but it also has to do with conditioned responses and unconscious stuff. If you have a lot of trauma in your life, such as major birth trauma, being abused as a child, major losses, serious illnesses or injuries to overcome, drug addictions, dysfunctional family, etc., you are going to have more work to do than someone who has had an ideal life. Instead of feeling and acting like a victim, however, it would be healthier to recognize that at some level you must be really strong because you've picked some major lessons to learn in life. Maybe you needed to prove to yourself that you were a survivor.

With few exceptions, when you have major life issues to overcome, you're going to need some professional help in getting through them. Find yourself a therapist or join a self-help group, but be sure the focus is positive. Don't get into a situation where the whole focus is on problems or where it's a gripe session. You already have a bunch of problems, and you don't need to reinforce them further or learn how to be a better complainer. That will only strengthen your victimhood. In order to solve a problem, you must focus on a solution, not on the problem itself. Doesn't that make intuitive sense to you?

In therapy, the best approach will combine cognitive instruction (learning to think effectively), some behavioral therapy, and possibly some hypnosis or relaxation training. There is a whole field now of "positive psychology" that was not around when I did my training, but that is the type of therapy I intuitively did on my own. Inner child work was popular in the late eighties and in the nineties, which was quite helpful if the person had major emotional wounds as a child, but you have to be sure the therapist doesn't get you stuck at that level. Rediscovering your inner child can be wonderful, unless you use it as an excuse to not grow up. There is a big difference between being childlike and having a sense of wonder, versus being a spoiled brat and expecting others to cater to your needs.

All effective therapy should teach self-responsibility. You are the only one who can be responsible for changing yourself. The therapist is only a guide or teacher. As I've said before, it is all about choices—choosing to be responsible for your life or choosing, instead, to be a victim. I would suggest that you choose a therapist who understands the balance of mind, body, and spirit.

In your quest toward happiness, you need to find some clarity on what makes you happy. If you think it is all about power, wealth, status, material things, and outer beauty, you've got some really distorted ideas. That's what the awakening is all about—

the recognition that these are not the things that bring happiness in life. What brings happiness is an inner conscious awareness of your higher self and discovering that we are all connected. You might call it cosmic consciousness. This is the foundation for experiencing real joy in your life.

3

Spirit Is

Some time ago, when NBC aired a television program called "Ancient Prophecies" during prime time, it was so popular they received over 24,000 telephone calls and sold over 50,000 video copies of the program. It was soon followed by "Ancient Prophecies II, III, and IV," "Prophecies 2000," "Ancient Mysteries," etc. Why the sudden interest in future events as foretold in the past? Why are we frequently hearing of things that in the recent past would have blown our minds, such as angels, miracles, manifestations, ETs, alien abductions, possession or entity attachment, secret governments, impending earth changes, faces and pyramids on Mars, ancient civilizations with advanced technologies, whales and dolphins as advanced life forms, the Sasquatch People, reincarnation and past-life therapy, polar shifts, and mass ascension? Has the whole world gone mad?

Quite the contrary. The interest in these unusual topics is a direct result of a major shift in consciousness. The fascination with such things is an indication of a great spiritual awakening. The shift in consciousness is affecting the whole world, and the bottom line during these extraordinary times is that we must learn to choose love over fear. It's really that simple.

Many master teachers are presently positioned to help people through this shift. I've had the privilege of working with a few along the way. Some are very advanced in their presentations. Essentially, they're teaching "graduate school." It's my task, though, to teach the beginning courses; and I believe the educational process needs to be fun, even if the topics are sometimes heavy. A spiritual path is much easier when you maintain a sense of humor.

The real "heavies" during these times will likely be the professional skeptics who will continue to argue for our limitations. Some of them will be scientists and traditional "hellfire-and-damnation" ministers. They have the most to lose because they have so completely bought into the accepted view of reality. However, there are those from even these esteemed professions who are awakening to the fact that what we have been led to believe for so long is not true. This limited understanding of reality is crumbling before our eyes. Science, religion, governments, financial institutions—everything we have held near and dear—are all going through drastic changes, and so are we.

Our world, as we have known it, is about to be turned upside down—perhaps literally during a polar shift—but it is all for a greater purpose. We are experiencing the labor pains of a wonderful new world coming into being, the culmination of a plan that was put in place thousands of years ago. We aren't even into hard labor yet, but we need to prepare for it. The best part about this amazing birth process is that we are right in the labor room with ringside seats to observe something miraculous. An extraordinary new world is being born. So sit down, hold on, and pass the popcorn. It's going to be a great show, and the greatest part of this is awakening to spirit.

There is a misunderstanding about "spirit" and what it means to be spiritual. Some people immediately associate it with religion or going to church, but being religious and being spiritual are two completely different things. Being religious implies an association with one or more of the world's religions. There is a structure, specific dogma, and beliefs. A religious person may or may not be pious or dogmatic, and a religious person may or may not be spiritual.

Likewise, a person may be very spiritual, but not part of any particular religion. A spiritual person seeks a sense of connection, whether that is with God, Jesus, nature, his or her own higher self, or the spirit world in a broader sense—guides, ascended masters, or the angelic realm. Such spirituality is an individual experience and usually does not involve any specific structure or dogma, which is just a system of doctrines believed to be true.

My own spiritual journey has run the gamut from being raised Presbyterian to a later appreciation for metaphysical mysticism. I was even a Sufi for six years, which is more of a mystical philosophy than a specific religion. It is Islamic mysticism, but most people know of it through Rumi, the great Sufi mystic and poet. Presently, I just feel a connection with "All That Is"—a Oneness that I experience as God. When I was young there were times I felt certain biases toward other systems of religious expression, but I now understand the underlying connection of all religions and also the need for diversity. A great master teacher once said that the many religions were as individual pearls in a beautiful necklace, and God was the thread that ran through them—the thread that held it all together. I think it might have been Paramahansa Yogananda who said that. Personally, I believe the overall connection is love. In saying that, I am also reminded of the Biblical verse, "God is love."

The religious similarities are far greater than any differences which is also true of human beings. If we would just focus on similarities instead of differences, maybe we would consciously evolve much more rapidly:

Christianity—*Do unto others as you would have them do unto you* (Matthew 7.12).

Judaism—*What you do not wish for yourself, do not wish for others* (Talmud Shabbat 31.A).

Islam—*No one will be a true believer unless he wishes for others what he wishes for himself* (Sunnatt).

Buddhism—*Do not offend others as you would not like to be offended* (Udanavarga 5.18).

Brahmanism—*Never do unto others what would hurt you if done unto you* (Mahabharata 5.15).

Confucianism—*What we do not wish to be done to us, let us not do it to others* (Analects 15.23).

Taoism—*Make as yours the profits of your fellowman as well as his loss* (Tai-shang Kin-ying P'ien).

Maya—*You are myself. We are all one* (Popol Vuh).

Bahai Faith—*If you seek justice choose for others what you would choose for yourself* (The Bayan).

(Above list from "Cosmic Disclosure," David Wilcock, Gaia Television.)

Presently, there is a tremendous leap of consciousness taking place on this planet, causing a great interest in spirituality and self-awareness. You see this in popular literature like *The Secret* by Rhonda Byrne and other similar books as well. Many of the major publishing houses have whole divisions that cater to spiritual literature. In the 1990s I remember trying to locate metaphysical literature in local bookstores, and I would never know whether they would be under religion, philosophy, astrology, or the occult. Now, there are many Internet sites, television programs, publishers, and numerous resources for spiritual versus religious interests. My favorite right now is Gaia Television over the Internet with numerous categories, i.e., metaphysics, paranormal, ancient wisdom, Yoga, etc.

I have been on the spiritual path since early childhood. I remember as a young child imagining frequently that I was walking hand-in-hand with Jesus. In early grade school, maybe the first or second grade, I remember memorizing Bible verses in Sunday school at the Hollywood Presbyterian Church, to earn my own Bible. At Forest Home, a lovely Christian conference center in the San Bernardino mountains of Southern California, I loved to sit in the small, log chapel that was donated to Forest Home by my grandparents, Grace and Clarence Cook—Nana and Papa to me.

I remained active in the church until my early twenties, when I had a falling out with mainstream Presbyterianism because I saw them dragging their feet on issues of importance to me—civil rights and the war in Vietnam. I also managed to become involved in a minor scandal when the youth minister and I fell in love after working closely together for two years.

My father was a trustee in the church, and my mother was in the choir. I was a counselor and teacher for the high school kids. The minister and I were much too naïve at that time to actually have an affair. It was more like two teenagers innocently stealing a kiss once in a while. Ultimately, though, we both ended up separating from our spouses. After that, the relationship eventually became sexual. However, we only continued our involvement for a short time before I rebelled against traditional religion altogether and left the relationship. I now recognize that time as one of the major turning points in my life. I decided to become a single student rather than becoming a minister's wife.

By then, I had begun my college career as a single parent, which concluded ten years later with a Ph.D. in clinical psychology from the University of Washington. Most of those years, 1968 through 1978, I identified with the "flower children," but I was also a responsible "A" student with two kids to raise, so I wasn't exactly a hippy. It was an interesting time of sexual exploration and freedom that extended to the social culture as a whole. I shifted away from traditional religion, but eventually came full-circle toward a much greater sense of spirituality, after a period of religious abstinence.

An important spiritual awakening came in 1977, in a rather unique way. I had decided to attend a past-life regression seminar in Seattle taught by Dick Sutphen, who was in the early stages of his very successful career as a seminar leader, author, and producer of metaphysical self-help audio and video tapes. I was one of several people chosen for a demonstration because of our ability to experience hypnosis easily. He told us to privately focus on a problem we wanted to solve. He worked with us as a group, but when he touched our foreheads and counted to three, we would know he was speaking directly to us in that moment, as an individual.

As Dick worked with each person, I could hear each one experiencing something quite profound. One was being attacked by a wolf, another was speaking in a childlike voice to an abusive mother. I became concerned that their experiences were so vivid, Dick might get to me and nothing would happen.

When Dick touched my forehead and counted to three, I immediately felt my heart begin to beat more rapidly. The physical reaction took me by surprise. Trying to interpret my experience internally, I said, "I seem to be afraid."

"You needn't be afraid," he said. "You can experience this as an objective observer."

Then I said, "I seem to be burning." Tears were running down my cheeks. I went on to describe being burned as a witch as a young woman. I was twenty years old, and I had long, blonde hair. I was accused of being a witch because I communicated with animals. It seemed to be a church that was responsible, and when I focused on the church leader, I realized it was the same minister I had briefly been involved with in this lifetime, during my early twenties. Later, I thought about the fact that he may have burned me in a past life, but I had burned him in this life by leaving the relationship.

The outcome of that experience, which actually only lasted a few minutes, was that I recognized my anger toward institutionalized religion came from more than just my personal experiences in the Presbyterian church. I learned that we are affected by not only those things we experience in this life, but also by all those things we experienced in past lives, as well. This allowed me to have a significant breakthrough spiritually because I forgave the past, let go of my anger against the church, and came into an acceptance that people seek out whatever spiritual approach is appropriate for them. That is why there needs to be religious diversity, and it's not for us to judge what another chooses. I also recognized that relationship as a karmic lesson and the importance of forgiveness. Since that time, I have guided hundreds of past-life regressions for clients, and I've seen people make dramatic changes, sometimes after only one session.

When I work with clients in this way, I tell them it is not necessary to believe in reincarnation. The technique is powerful because it elicits a story that comes from within the person, and I never know ahead of time just what will evolve. The story might be a real past-life experience, a fantasy, or a dream-like sequence. However, where it comes from is not as important as the fact that people can make major changes in their attitude and behavior through "re-living" and releasing what are frequently traumatic events, although some regressions are gentle and quite beautiful. It depends on what is most important to the person at that time, on what is most affecting them at present.

One of the things that has caused such problems on this planet is that we have chosen to focus on differences rather than on similarities. We get caught up in whether a person is of a different religion, a different color, a different sex, a different nationality, instead of looking at the much larger picture—the fact that we are all human beings, we are all Earthlings. It is actually impossible to judge another because we have no idea what that person's real experience is. We can't see their past or feel their pain, but we can learn to have compassion, and we can learn to focus on our similarities. We are actually much more alike than different, and we are all being led into this planetary frequency shift together, which may be the thousand years of peace mentioned in the Bible or the Golden Age mentioned in *The Urantia Book* or maybe just a shift from the third dimension to a higher frequency as mentioned by some ET races. It will be a period of peace, joy, prosperity, and sacred serenity where we will awaken as the powerful spiritual beings we truly are—if we choose to do so.

It is imperative that we wake up to this understanding in whatever manner is appropriate for us because the planet is going through a dimensional shift; and if you aren't ready for it, you may have the very special opportunity of going through the third-dimensional stuff all over again. Think of it, do you really want to become a hairy barbarian again and start all over?

The fact is, though, everything will evolve in a perfect way. Each soul will get to experience exactly what is appropriate for that soul to evolve. We are eternal beings, and all of this is a process of growth. Personally, I plan to make the shift with the millions of others who are making that choice, whether they consciously realize it or not. In fact, I know that my own personal task here on Earth is to help others make that shift. Come on, guys, with the right attitude, it will be a great adventure.

When I use the term "spirit," I use it as a collective. I am referring to God or All That Is, and also to ascended masters, angels, our personal spirit guides, and so forth. Some people prefer to think in a specific way. The concept of angels may be comfortable to a more traditionally religious person, while spirit guides may be more acceptable to a person with a metaphysical orientation. Once again, we need not get so caught up in differences, or in determining who's right or who's wrong in their conceptualization. Instead, we need to recognize that each person is perceiving at his or her own level of comfort and understanding, and he or she is connecting with these loving beings in whatever way seems right. Besides, it is all a construct, just a way of perceiving what we think of as reality. We get in trouble when we confuse our particular construct with Truth.

The present explosive interest in angels is certainly no accident. We are awakening to the fact that we're not alone. One book on this topic, written by Brad Steiger, is called *Angels Over Their Shoulders*. The book is about children's encounters with these divine messengers. There truly are many levels of enlightened beings who want to assist us with our growth, and the angelic realm is one of them. Fortunately, because of our cultural history, we have a certain openness toward these magnificent beings.

However, there are other beings, too, that I include in my collective understanding of spirit. Personal guidance comes from loving and wise beings who assist us in our personal development. What we sometimes think of as our "conscience" is frequently a communication with these guides. The greatest difficulty most guides have is being underemployed. They may sit by the "phone," but it never rings. If most people don't even have awareness of their existence, they aren't going to seek their help. In this case, ignorance is certainly not bliss. Instead, it's a significant handicap.

There are a number of ways you can get more in touch with your guidance. The first is to simply ask for their help. This can be done in a prayerful manner or it can be more secular, i.e., "Hey, guys, if you're here, let's talk." At first you'll feel your telepathic communication is just your own thoughts as you start to have dialogues in your mind. However, with practice, you will eventually begin to distinguish your thoughts from guidance. The best way to become more receptive to this is to learn to quiet your mind by practicing some form of meditation. Most people in our culture know at least something about prayer, which is talking to God. However, they know very little about being in a place of peace where they still their minds enough to listen to God. Meditation is a way to learn how to listen, and it helps to release the stress from our everyday lives.

Another category of beings are the ascended masters. These beings may or may not have lived Earthly lives, because there are extraterrestrial ascended masters. Regardless of where they originated, they reached a state of divine understanding and connection, then they ascended. This means they did not experience what we think of as the usual death cycle. Instead they raised the vibration of their bodies and took the body with them into a higher dimension. To a normal third-dimensional being, this would look as though they turned into light and just disappeared. Jesus is, of course, a wonderful example of an ascended being, although most people believe he went through a death cycle first. There are many others, as well. They form what is known as the Great White Brotherhood, which is not very politically correct, but it implies white light, not a racial category, and there are sisters, too. One book that goes into more detail is *The Complete Ascension Manual*, by Dr. David Stone.

It could take many lifetimes to completely understand this topic of ascension, and there are varying theories about what it means in terms of the present shift on this planet. However, my immediate intention is to introduce you to the collective I call Spirit. We must also include God. Although I was raised with the concept of God being a loving, wise father figure on a throne, this is not at all the way I presently think of God. It is fine to conceptualize God in whatever way works for you, but don't assume your way is the absolute truth or your way of thinking is the way everyone else should think. That arrogant belief has caused a lot of separation and many wars.

Some people who have had bad experiences with religion might be more comfortable with just adding another "o" and thinking of God as Good. I did that for a while during my rebellious period toward institutional religion. You can also reinterpret Jesus as Christ Consciousness for the same reason, if that feels more comfortable to you. As I said earlier, I have come to think of God as All That Is or the Oneness. That feels best to me; but when I pray, I use the term, "Mother/Father God." That term addresses both the feminine and masculine aspects of God.

Many traditionally raised individuals criticize other religions because they have "many gods," not realizing they are merely aspects of one God. A man might be a father, a husband, a son, a lover, an employee, etc., but these are aspects or expressions of the one man. When I learned this, it was a tremendous help in understanding other religions.

I also now think of God much more as a force or an energy, rather than as a being. I believe this Primary Force is Love. I am not talking about the usual human love that is possessive or selfish, but a divine love that is unconditional. During these rapidly changing and evolving times, we are meant to learn about unconditional love, which is a major part of making the dimensional shift—going from third to a higher density—which is a frequency shift. Everything is frequency, and our planet and beings upon it are rising in frequency which is a good thing, not a bad thing.

This has been a basic introduction to what I mean as Spirit in the collective. There is a whole other category, though, that I have alluded to. Not only are there many interdimensional beings, but there are also extraterrestrial beings. These are not mutually exclusive categories. ET's are also interdimensional beings, as are we up to a point. Traveling interdimensionally just has to do with raising or lowering your frequency or vibration. Shaman frequently do this during a healing procedure. The most important thing about all this is to realize that we are definitely not alone in the cosmos.

4

WE ARE NOT ALONE

ACCEPTING THE PRESENCE of extraterrestrials can be quite difficult, especially if you have bought into the great lie on the part of our government. Most other countries are now much more open about their UFO and ET files and have put information onto the Internet, but there is so much that our government still holds back; and because of all the lies over so many years, people will not know what to believe as word gets out.

As you read these next two chapters, many of you will question what I say. "How does she know this?" you'll ask. "These things can't possibly be true. It sounds like science fiction to me." The fact is that reality is more incredible than science fiction. I will give you many resources so you can check these things out for yourself, but I will not defend the truth. If you want to think of this as just an interesting story, that's fine with me. I learned long ago not to try to prove things to others because people see what they want to see or what they are capable of understanding, depending on their present level of conscious awareness.

Anyone who is serious about seeking real knowledge of UFOs and/or ETs will convince themselves of the reality of their existence with as little as a few hours of legitimate study, but you have to look in the right places. When I heard the late Carl Sagan saying there was no evidence for the existence of extraterrestrial spacecraft visiting this planet, I was amazed. He was obviously an intelligent, educated man. However, he was either purposely or naively making statements based on prejudice. Personally, my sense is that Dr. Sagan was not as naïve as he sometimes appeared. I'll leave that for the reader to determine. My guess is that his private opinion differed from his public opinion, for whatever reason.

There are now so many resources it is hard to know where to begin. There is an annual conference now held in Phoenix that brings legitimate researchers from all over the world. It is in February each year, and it is called the International UFO Congress (www.ufocongress.com). Each year they have numerous speakers, and the talks are all available on DVD. One of my favorite speakers is Jaime Maussan from Mexico. He is like the Dan Rather of Mexico and has more film and information than almost anyone alive. Another resource is Stan Romanek who wrote the book, *Messages*, about his very documented contact experiences (www.stanromanek.com). Dr. C. B. Scott Jones and Dr. Angela T. Smith wrote *Voices From The Cosmos* about their telepathic ET communications.

There are hundreds of good books on the topics of ETs and UFOs.

Our planet has been visited regularly from elsewhere for thousands of years, and it's not a question of whether they come from outer space or from inside the Earth or whether they are interdimensional because it's not a mutually exclusive situation. The answer is "all of the above." There are real physical ships out there that leave landing traces. They can go in and out of large bodies of water, and they have been seen going into the Earth. It is possible they are entering some sort of holographic portal in some instances.

They are definitely interdimensional, as are we, with proper training. One of the reasons the UFOs are often seen making right-angle turns is because that is part of the technique used to make a dimensional shift. This is also why many people have seen them just disappear. They leave our range of visibility. It's also why ETs can walk through walls or suddenly appear in a room, although sometimes this is just high technology. A frequency shift is not at all difficult for them, but for us it takes a bit of practice because we are too dense, literally and figuratively.

If you are a hard-core scientific type and want to understand this, you need to study a field of knowledge known as sacred geometry. In 1994, I studied for nine days in Austin, Texas, with a Master Teacher known as Drunvalo Melchizedek. However, unless you are willing to accept that the world is not as you have believed it to be, you will have difficulty getting through your own prejudice to the real knowledge that is available. You must expand your beliefs if you want to see more, rather than saying, "I'll believe it when I see it." There were approximately ninety people from around the world at the "Flower of Life Workshop." At that time Drunvalo was working on a book that was to come out in two volumes. I must warn you, though, his teachings are not for the faint-of-heart. They are very advanced and exceptionally enlightening.

Not only have I studied UFOs extensively, but I have had my own conscious experiences. There are also some experiences I have had in the past that have come into full conscious awareness through hypnosis. I am not an "armchair researcher" in this field. For over a year, I was the Las Vegas working group coordinator for CSETI (Center for the Study of Extraterrestrial Intelligence). I also served on their executive council for two very active years.

Many of us who are helping others understand these times of great change have had tremendous assistance from extraterrestrial sources either directly or telepathically. Some of these beings have come from what we think of as our future, to help us through the challenging times directly ahead of us and to welcome us into the galactic community.

My own instruction from ETs began in childhood, at least during this present lifetime. I have a vivid memory of being a toddler watching a bright, bluish-white light in my backyard, which was in Glendale, California. I remember floating out through the window into a ship where I was gently escorted to an area where I could see a control panel on my left in the background. I sat across a table from three beings who looked at me in a kind and loving manner. They were short and frail with large heads and large eyes, and one of them was a bit taller than the other two. I had my hands outstretched in front of me over the table, and I giggled because I thought my new found playmates were going to play "patty-cake" with me. Instead, a blue ball appeared several inches above my hands. It was a hologram of the planet Earth. As far as I know, my lessons began at this time, lessons about our beautiful home planet, Terra.

I have no conscious awareness at present of exactly what that lesson comprised. However, I do know that I had a keen interest from childhood in UFOs, ETs, other unusual phenomena, and an understanding and expectation regarding major earth changes. I suspect now that my unusual interest in these things began with that experience on the ship when I was around two years old.

This memory of my childhood connection with ETs emerged through a vivid hypnotic regression experience in the fall of 1992. However, the next memory I am going to describe came up spontaneously into conscious awareness in 1976 or 1977. I was in graduate school at the time, living in Seattle. I was just walking through my living room one day when I suddenly had the vivid image flash into my mind of looking down from a rocky hillside to the desert floor below. There was a small disc-shaped craft resting on a tripod with two humanoid beings underneath wearing silvery space suits. They had helmets on their heads that looked like an upturned fishbowl. Over to my left was an adult figure, a man in casual clothing wearing a red plaid flannel shirt. I realized it was my father, and I was about eight years old.

My first reaction to this peculiar image that had spontaneously popped into my mind was, "What the hell was that?" I decided it must have been a dream I had as a child, and I didn't think much more about it for several years. In June of 1980, however, I began my professional work in ufology, and I connected with two pioneering researchers, both known for their exceptional work with hypnotic regression.

Dr. Leo Sprinkle is a psychologist who was at that time the director of the Counseling Center at the University of Wyoming. Presently, he is an emeritus professor doing private practice and research in Laramie. The late Dr. James Harder was a professor of hydraulic and civil engineering in the University of California system at Berkeley. He passed away in 2006, but he had been an emeritus professor and the founder of The Society for the Advancement of Civilization.

I met these two esteemed colleagues at a small, private gathering of UFO researchers in Las Vegas. I happened to mention to them the vivid image I had spontaneously recalled a few years previously. They suggested we do a hypnotic regression to explore it further. This regression experience allowed me to fill in the details. I was eight years old, and we were on a family vacation in the Mammoth Mountain area near Bishop, in Northern California. During that time, we went to Lake Mary every summer because friends of my parents owned the Lake Mary Lodge. Since cars were not air conditioned then, we usually drove across the desert in the night or early morning hours.

I'm not sure why we originally stopped the car, whether we had seen lights or something else that attracted us to the site. It seemed evident, though, that my mother, older sister, and younger brother remained in the car in a motionless state, while my father and I investigated. I don't remember anything beyond viewing the craft and the two beings underneath, and I'm not sure if anything else came out in the regression because that was a long time ago, and I didn't get it on tape. However, both Dr. Harder and Dr. Sprinkle thought it was a real experience I had as a child, not just a dream.

Some time ago while visiting my mother in LaVerne, California, we were watching a television show about UFOs. I asked her if she remembered anything happening on any of our family vacations to Lake Mary. She said, "One time there were unusual lights in the desert, that I remember." I was quite surprised by her response and wished I had checked it out with my father before he died. He might have surprised me, too, with an interesting memory.

In January of 1994, I attended a small, private gathering of UFO researchers at Dr. Steven Greer's home in Asheville, North Carolina. Dr. Greer is the international director of CSETI. Command Sergeant Major, Bob Dean, a retired military officer, showed some of his slides after dinner. I was quite surprised to see an image of an alien—I prefer to call them the visitors—that looked just like the two I had seen as a child underneath the disc-shaped ship. It was a drawing of a being with a humanoid shape in a suit that had puffy rolls of material, especially noticeable on the arms and legs of the suit. Even the helmet was the same. It was the first time I had ever seen anything similar to my recollection. Bob Dean is one of the more articulate speakers on the subject of government knowledge about UFOs, and I was very pleased to meet him in this informal setting, along with his wife, Cecilia.

Another hypnotic regression experience took place in December of 1993, when Dr. Harder, once again, was visiting Las Vegas to attend a UFO conference. He used hypnosis to regress me to approximately the age of twelve. I was riding my horse, Lady, in the foothills of Arcadia, California, something I did often at that age. She was the first of four horses I had as a child and was a beautiful, sorrel-colored Tennessee Walker with a flaxen mane and tail. I tied her to a tree and was then taken aboard a ship where I underwent what seemed like a routine evaluation regarding my progress in school. They were pleased that I was doing so well as a student, but I was impatient at the time because I was concerned about Lady. It was just the sort of thing that would have disturbed me at that age. My horses meant more to me than anything else in the world, and I took their welfare very seriously.

After the regression, I told Dr. Harder I had known from a very young age that I was to be some sort of scientist, before I even knew what a scientist was. I now realize I had been programmed from an early age to get an education and an advanced degree because it was going to be important in my future work. My education was like an obsession to me. I put it above all else and made many sacrifices, as did my children, to get that Ph.D.

All the other experiences I have had with UFOs as an adult have been fully awake, fully conscious—at least as far as I presently remember. A number of my UFO sightings have been witnessed by others, as well. My experiences are too numerous to mention in detail, but the most extraordinary sighting was on a CSETI research mission to Mexico in January of 1993.

Five well-trained field researchers, including Dr. Greer, spent six days in the volcanic region east of Mexico City. We were in a remote area near a small village on the east side of Mt. Popocatepetl, the fourth largest volcano in the world, when a large triangle-shaped ship approached us at a low altitude. We had been doing "coherent thought sequencing," a meditative technique where we had our eyes closed while Dr. Greer verbally guided us out into space to connect with the visitors. Suddenly, he intuitively knew to open his eyes and look in a particular direction. He emphatically said, "This is the real thing, guys," as he pointed toward the north side of Mt. Popo—our nickname for the volcano.

The ship immediately turned in our direction as Dr. Greer flashed it with a bright searchlight. It at first appeared to be a large amber light. As it approached, it descended even further in our direction and flashed us with lights in response to our light flashes, both on approach and as it departed and disappeared behind a low ridge directly northeast of our location. As soon as it turned the underside toward us, I could see the shape was a triangle. I shouted, "It's the triangle ship!" There were three white lights, one in each corner, and a red, pulsing light in the center.

This is the same type of ship that was reportedly seen in Belgium. Although it was quite large—at least the size of a 747, if not larger—it made no noise, and it came toward us about at the speed of a single engine plane. It was an awesome experience for all of us on the team, but none of us were fearful. Instead, we were animated and excited. We thought it might land because it was coming lower and lower, and the lights on the edge of the ship looked like landing lights.

The same ship, or one just like it, appeared at the exact same time, 11:45 p.m., the following night. This time it approached us from the east instead of from the north, and it once again showed the underside with the triangular light formation; but it was higher in the sky. It was flying from east to west, toward the volcano. All our sightings were relatively low to the ground, especially the first one, and we speculated that the ETs were doing some sort of geological research because of the volcano. It is a geologically active area, and there have been other ship sightings around the world close to volcanoes.

Everyone always asks, "Did you get pictures?" We were trained researchers, and we had lots of high-priced equipment with us at the time—a video camera on a tripod, a 35mm camera on a tripod, a 35mm snapshot camera, numerous sets of binoculars, field lights for signaling, strobe lights to mark a landing site, and a radar device. We had been taking pictures with the expensive camera earlier in the evening by the light of a very full moon, however, when the ship was closest to us, all three of our cameras failed. I observed another teammate pushing the button repeatedly on her snapshot camera with no results. As soon as the ship went behind the ridge, it suddenly worked.

We were uncertain whether the malfunctioning cameras were the victims of a purposeful "jamming," possibly because they did not want to be documented at that time or whether it was just electromagnetic effects from the proximity of the ship. The sound on the video camera also shut off, but only during the time of closest interaction. Our radar device did not go off as it should have, but it did go off once after the second night in the field. We were just leaving the site at about 3:30 a.m., there was no ship in sight, but it went off just as we were driving back to the main road from the farmer's field where we had spent the night. It felt like some sort of acknowledgment from the visitors of our presence. We were in the middle of nowhere, and the radar device did not go off at any other time.

We had numerous other sightings and anomalous experiences on that trip, including a close-up daytime sighting of a small craft by myself and two other team members. For a moment we caught sight of a silvery craft near the volcano. It looked like tinfoil reflecting sunlight. The craft went behind a cloud after only a few seconds. I would estimate it was as close as one-quarter mile to one-half mile distance from us, and between 500 and 1,000 feet of altitude. It made no noise, and from my angle of sight, it appeared like a small tube angling up toward the volcano, like a small plane taking off. However, it had no wings, no tail, no markings, and if it was a conventional craft, it would have crashed into the side of the 18,000-foot volcano. There were no airports in the area, only remote fields and hills—we had just hiked the whole area two days previously. I suspect it was a small disc I was viewing from the side. Another team member saw portholes, and I noticed he had exceptional vision when we were doing our night fieldwork later that evening, so I trust his impression was accurate.

I realize I have had extraordinary experiences related to UFOs and ETs compared to most people, but I know I am not alone in this. Whitley Strieber's book, *The Secret School*, describes in detail his personal interactions with the visitors. There are many of us who have been taught by ETs since childhood, many others who have had telepathic communication with ETs (*Voices From The Cosmos* by C. B. Scott Jones, Ph.D. and Angela T. Smith, Ph.D.). Some others have taken part in genetic research, not always to their liking. My sense of this, though, is that we have only a glimpse of the larger picture.

There may be a far greater meaning beyond our present understanding of these celestial visitations. It is likely the visitors are related to our "Creator Gods," and some of them may prove to be our "saviors," if during future events we need to be temporarily lifted from the planet. However, we must first learn to conquer our fear. In *Breakthrough*, another book by Whitley Strieber, he writes, "I feel strongly that fear is the key thing that prevents us from living the richer, more vital life that is implied by this whole experience." He has a lot to say in his book about what that fear in regard to the visitors is all about.

5

The Visitors

MANY OF YOU have no doubt heard about "alien abductions." They have even sometimes made it into the funny paper and on popular cartoon programs, i.e., "South Park." Mulder on "The X Files" was obsessed with the abduction of his sister when they were children. It is almost impossible to be unaware of this topic if you watch prime-time television. There was a time when I thought that abductions had something to do with the evolution of our species. I thought it was a cooperative effort, even if the individuals involved did not remember their agreement to assist in this important genetic research project. In some cases this may still be the case.

However, I now feel that there is more to the story, so to speak, in that some abductees report the negative involvement of our military personnel. Regardless of where you stand on the issue of "free will" versus "violation," an older but excellent book on this topic is *Abductions*, by the late Dr. John Mack who was a controversial Harvard psychiatrist. He didn't just focus on fear and sensationalism, but instead he reported the abductees' experiences in a much broader context. It is a mistake to focus only on fear-based perceptions, whether we are dealing with ETs or humans, although fear is a natural human response under the circumstances.

In the past, I heard of one abduction case where the couple involved were *asked* if they would participate. It was an Indian couple in Ecuador. The husband was first approached by the ETs, and was asked if his wife might agree to help them. She agreed to do so after several days of thinking about it, and they were together through the artificial insemination procedure. Several months later, they were again together when the fetus was removed. They felt they had participated in important research, and it was a positive experience for both of them.

There is another person, Stan Romanek, who has been taken many times and has been involved in a genetic program, as well. He has written about it in his book, *Messages: The World's Most Documented Extraterrestrial Contact Story*. He has even met some of his hybrid children, as have others involved in the various genetic programs. Stan's wife has also written her version of his abductions in that he is usually taken from their bedroom. Her book is called, *From My Side of the Bed*. Most interesting, though, is the fact that he was unexpectedly also given a surgery on his knee at one time which solved the problem right before he was scheduled to have surgery with his doctor. More recently, people have been attacking his claims and trying to discredit him, but that is not uncommon when someone is writing about what others view as paranormal events.

In the book, *Above Black*, Dan Sherman explains how his mother was abducted before he was born. His birth was genetically manipulated to give him specific characteristics later utilized when he was in the Air Force. A senior officer met with him privately to tell him about the research in the early 1960s. He told him there had been a connection with this particular group of ETs since 1947. This genetic manipulation would allow Dan to assist worldwide communications if a time came in the future when our communication systems were inoperative; possibly a polar shift, magnetic changes on Earth, war, other serious earth changes, etc. Dan took part in a specific training program to develop his mind for this work. The most interesting part of the story is that Dan's mother had been told by doctors she would not be able to have children. He believes he was born because of the ETs work and owes his life to them.

I realize that not all the many ET races who have visited this planet have had our best interests in mind, just as we as a nation did not have the best interests of others in mind when we engaged in slavery, murdered the Native Americans and stole their land, took part in wars for economic gain, and polluted our planet. However, I purposely choose to focus on the need for a diplomatic liaison with all ETs, rather than a good guy/bad guy scenario. We certainly have diplomacy with other nations on our planet with whom we don't agree all the time. The need is even greater with ETs because this is the beginning of our planet becoming part of the intergalactic community, and we need all the help we can get from those who might offer a higher awareness and a broader perspective on our planetary evolution. I imagine an organization known as the "Global Galactic League of Nations" which already exists, according to Corey Goode with the Sphere Alliance ("Cosmic Disclosure," Gaia Television).

Because "like attracts like" a small segment of our military has become involved with a specific group of ETs. This group of ETs has exchanged technological information for permission to do the genetic research. We have a much higher level of technology than the common man knows about. I suspect we would have received more assistance long ago with other pressing human concerns, i.e., feeding our people, abolishing disease, creating greater harmony among the races and nationalities, if we had not come from such a military mind-set. That is the challenge for our future, to change our orientation to one of universal peace and heightened spiritual awareness.

In the meantime, this elite group some call the "secret government," along with similar groups from Russia, England, and possibly elsewhere, have been working with ETs for over sixty years or maybe longer. It is unfortunate that we have felt the need to keep it all top-secret, but the decision to do so was made by men with a military mind-set, and it was initiated at a time in history when there was great fear about Communism. There was also the fear of public panic based on the "War of the Worlds" scenario. Orson Welles' radio show freaked out many listeners in the 1930s. One of my editors, Faye Frost, remembers hearing this show on the radio as a little girl. Her aunt called in terror and said, "The Martians have landed!" She had to explain to her aunt that it was just a radio show.

Various factions of our government have worked on these top-secret projects in New Mexico, Nevada, California, Australia, and probably other locations, as well. Many of the UFOs seen in our skies are related to this work, especially near Area 51 here in Southern Nevada, north of Las Vegas. Personally, I think this base became more of a decoy in recent years. I suspect that many top-secret projects have been moved to Pine Gap in Australia, and other locations.

Some of the individuals who have worked on these projects have been given limited permission to discuss their work. A former friend of mine is one of these individuals. He was a retired mechanical engineer who worked on a disc-shaped simulator at Los Alamos, New Mexico, and in Area 51. I believe this new openness is a preparation for an eventual public announcement about ETs by our government. Many other governments are already quite open about the Visitors, but they are waiting for the United States to take a leading role in the dissemination of this information. Japan planned to open a UFO/ET museum that was supposed to have a grand opening event on July 4th, 1996. Shortly before the event took place, they changed their minds. Apparently, some people in our government didn't want a worldwide media event to take place at that time, and they influenced Japan to cancel the planned event. When the museum eventually opened, it was mostly a normal space museum in Hakui City, Japan, but it is not what it was originally intended to be.

For many years a small group of individuals made decisions about how to deal with the "ET/UFO problem." There were individual members from industry, science, and the military. Some people called this group "Majestic

12." Early on it was decided to use ridicule and disinformation as a means of handling UFO reports. Unfortunately, it takes time to override that approach, especially with journalists and scientists. I may be subjected to this tactic, as well, once this book is published. However, the approach isn't working very well anymore because too many people have had their own experiences, and many of them have recorded their sightings on video cameras and on smart phone videos. This is especially true in Mexico, Ecuador, New Mexico, Florida, and Japan.

One of the strategies for bringing this secret government/ET connection out into the open in the least harmful way has been through the use of the media, but for every positive movie there seems to be one aimed at causing fear. In the past we had "Close Encounters of the Third Kind" and "E.T." But there has also been "Independence Day," "District Nine," and "Alien." There were nightly television programs, as well, in the past: "The X-Files," "Sightings," and "Encounters." Fox network is bringing back "The X-Files" soon. That should be fun. Do you think they are trying to tell us something? Now, with the Internet available to almost everyone, there is a vast array of programming, both positive and negative.

I am quite concerned, though, with the implications of the fear based movies and television programs. The effect of these movies is to create fear, especially fear of aliens. I believe we are being prepared for a star wars scenario as imagined by President Reagan when he said that we would all come together if we had a "common enemy" that threatened the Earth. However, that so-called enemy may only oppose the hidden power elite, not all of mankind. Once again I mention the Gaia Television program, "Cosmic Disclosure," because they talk about this in detail.

Another source of alien exposure has been through advertisements. Since I do not watch regular television, I can't give all the examples, but I know there have been numerous ads with an ET or UFO theme. An extraordinary printed ad in the mid-80s caused quite a stir in the UFO community. It was a two-page spread in the magazine, *Aviation Week and Space Technology*, advertising Amoco Corporation. It used a portrait of an ET in shadow that looked like the real thing, shot in a studio. The ad copy read, "Technology So Advanced It Will Help Answer Some Big Questions." That's pretty incredible and so was the photo.

The most interesting thing about this is what happened when I was routinely checking my resources. I had called the reference librarian at UNLV to get the phone number for Amoco and for the magazine. I wanted to be sure I had described this ad correctly. At Amoco, I left a message on the voice mail recorder for the man in advertising. His message said he was out of the office that day. He never returned my call. I also called *Aviation Week and Space Technology* and was referred to their advertising division in New York. I spoke to two women there who remembered the ad. They confirmed the approximate date and that it was for Amoco Corporation. They couldn't tell me, though, which volume it was even though they told me they received around two calls a year about that particular ad. I thanked them and felt pleased that I had at least confirmed the company, the approximate date, and the proper name of the magazine. I made those calls on a Friday.

First thing Monday morning, I received a phone call from the late Phillip Klass, who was on the editorial board of *The Skeptical Inquirer*. He was possibly the number one "debunker" in the country, and invariably he had been trotted out on all the talk shows to do his routine. He always said there was no valid scientific evidence for UFOs and/or ETs. I had watched him so many times and concluded he was part of the disinformation conspiracy. I wondered sometimes, though, whether he actually believed what he said or if he was just in denial based on personal experiences of an unconscious nature. No one could be in the know and say some of the ridiculous things he used to say.

At the time, though, I certainly sat up and took notice that I received a call from the infamous Mr. Klass. He was charming and gracious and fully explained to me that he had been with *Aviation Week and Space Technology* for over forty years—first as an editor, then as a senior editor, and now as a contributing editor. He wanted to assure me that when the ad originally caused a furor in the ufology community, he had personally checked with the ad agency and even spoke to the artist who made the model. He said the artist was surprised about the stir it had caused, but he didn't have access anymore to that information because it was buried among his voluminous materials.

In the meantime, I tracked down a copy of the photograph from the magazine ad. I could see tiny wrinkles in the eyelids, minute lines around the lips, a realistic texture to the skin, and even what appeared to be veins on the forearm, since the ET was holding up his four-fingered hand. The head was shaped exactly like the image of an ET on the poster done by my friend who had worked on secret projects for many years. It isn't the familiar large round head with wraparound black eyes; instead, it has two big bulges in the skull, more like very defined right and left hemispheres of the brain. In the ad and in the poster, the ET has four slender fingers, and large, round, doe-like eyes. In fact, the poster and the ad are identical, even down to the circular area on the side of the skull, which appears to be an ear of some sort.

The phone call from Mr. Klass alerted me to look more closely into this. As soon as I received it, rather than just a call back from one of the women I originally spoke with, I knew there was more to the story. I felt much more certain that it was a real ET that posed for that photograph. If not, the artist was certainly well informed about the appearance of this particular ET species.

The top-secret group of individuals making decisions about how to bring all this out into the open are not necessarily evil men and women as they are sometimes portrayed by some UFO researchers. They have been trying to determine over all these years the best way to bring it out with the least destructive effect on the world's governments, financial institutions, religions, and collective consciousness. That is why they have relied so heavily on more subtle approaches through the media—sort of a subliminal approach to prepare us gradually.

One concern is that there are those in the religious community who will use this as a fear-inducing control mechanism. Some religious leaders will proclaim that all ETs are devils or messengers of Satan. It is imperative that we guard against this type of reaction because it will only interfere with moving more easily into the frequency upgrade. Those who accept these limiting beliefs will be greatly hindered in their ability to make the dimensional shift, because if you are into fear instead of love, you just won't make it. Remember the caveman scenario? Is that what you would prefer to a higher dimension? Think twice before choosing fear even if that has been your previous religious orientation. Your ultimate destiny depends upon the emotional choice you make now.

There is so much more going on behind the scenes with the "secret government," the military (mostly the Navy), the CIA (Central Intelligence Agency), NSA (National Security Agency), NASA (National Aeronautics and Space Administration), ONI (Office of Naval Intelligence), and the SSP (Secret Space Program). There is also a lot going on with ET advocacy groups like The Sphere Alliance, CSETI (Center for the Study of Extraterrestrial Intelligence), and even with the ETs themselves.

I believe the ETs that work with our government have actually wanted the secrecy maintained for their own reasons. I also suspect that joint ventures are happening on the moon and on Mars that would blow our minds, as wild as that may sound. Corey Goode confirms this in his interviews with David Wilcock on "Cosmic Disclosure."

We live in an Orwellian reality, but most people don't see what is happening because they are asleep spiritually and mentally. They are zoned out in front of TV with a beer in their hands, buying into the accepted view of reality. There are so many men and boys, and even some girls and women, who are addicted to video games. The young people, especially, can't be without their cell phones. This is very convenient for the powers-that-be who would just as soon have us stay asleep spiritually and consciously, because we are much easier to control under those conditions. There is far greater control in our country than some other supposedly more restrictive regimes, and much of it is information control.

Fortunately, a much higher power exists. We will not be allowed to totally destroy ourselves or the planet this time around. It isn't productive to get caught into the idea of "conspiracy" either. Some fanatics, such as those involved in the Oklahoma City bombing and the Twin Tower collapse, are all set to fight the secret government and expose them; but they don't realize that the two opposing factions are not the "good guys" and the "bad guys," as they see them. Instead, we are choosing sides based on whether we come from love-based or fear-based realities. If you decide to promote paranoia, even if it's true that a secret government runs things, you are playing on the wrong team. You are inadvertently aiding the side of darkness.

The dimensional shift is going to take place regardless of who is perceived to be in power. The field of ufology has for too long played into the conspiracy model. There is now a gradual shift, however, toward recognition that contact is related to consciousness. An excellent older book on just this topic is *Preparing for Contact*, by Lyssa Royal and Keith Priest. There was an important conference in June of 1996, held on an Indian reservation. It was about the "Star Beings" and had a strong spiritual focus, which is a step in the right direction. There was also an important release of information to coincide with the 50th anniversary of the Roswell crash. It was in the book, *The Day After Roswell,* and it was written by Col. Philip J. Corso, a retired Chief of the Army's Foreign Technology Division. He tells about his part in releasing alien artifacts for reverse-engineering projects which led to integrated circuit chips, lasers, and super-tenacity fibers. After that book was released, other people in industry came forward confirming the use of alien technology.

Several years ago, a popular radio personality, Art Bell, had been doing his nightly radio show, "Coast to Coast," during the week and "Dreamland" on Sunday nights. On January 5, 1998, he did a show he called "Disclosure." He interviewed a number of prominent individuals in the field of ufology and politics, including CSETI's Dr. Steven Greer. Dr. Greer told about his three-hour debriefing with the Director of Central Intelligence, James Woolsey, which took place in 1993. This was done during the time I was on the Executive Council of CSETI and it had been a big secret. These men being interviewed by Art Bell believed it was now time for everything to come out into the open. Obviously, that has continued to be a slow process.

On the same radio show, it was mentioned that Francis Barwood, a council woman from Phoenix at the time, was going to run for state office on a UFO platform. She is the woman who went through so much ridicule in 1997, when she asked for an investigation of the "Phoenix Lights." There had been a major sighting on March 13th, 1997, over the city of Phoenix of delta-shaped lights moving slowly and silently over the city. It was seen by hundreds of people. Eventually, the story was picked-up by major media in June after the political harassment of Francis Barwood reached epic proportions. A wonderful video was produced about this sighting by Stargate Productions called, "Lights Over Phoenix." (see Resources).

I believe the Visitors are moving us toward a new way of thinking.

We need to come together with respect for ourselves and for all life forms if we are going to gracefully enter and remain in the galactic community. I believe that earth changes and weather changes will help us come together, even if it is because we must do so for our survival. Humanity frequently rises above differences when confronted with trauma and disaster, becoming heroic and selfless in helping others. This degree of cooperation and assistance will happen much more easily if we learn to honor ourselves, others, and all life as a whole.

6

Honoring All Life

ALL OF LIFE serves us in so many ways, but we have lost track of that amidst the stresses and strains of existence. It's now time to serve others and not just ourselves. That is part of honoring all that is. The Buddhists know about this in their sense of reverence for all life on this planet. In this regard, many Christians are lagging behind, but they must reach this level within their consciousness in order to honor themselves. Presently, there is an issue with people crossing borders in this country and in Europe. This is to live a better life and to escape areas involved in war. We need to start thinking in terms of being earthlings helping other earthlings. We are all in this together whether we like it or not.

All sense of who we are begins with ourselves. If it is impossible for a person to love himself or herself, how can they love others? So many people think it's the opposite

Honoring All Life • 57

because they confuse the need to serve others as meaning they must deny themselves. This is not at all the way it is. You can't possibly serve others unless you are grounded in service to self. I am not talking about being self-centered in the negative sense, but about self-respect. When you respect yourself, you al

We are at a crossroads in our culture and on our planet. We are empowered now to awaken to who we really are, but so many are still sleeping. That is the challenge, to awaken ourselves first, then to awaken others. The fact is, we already know what we need to know. It isn't about reading more books, going to seminars, finding a guru. The time for all that is over. Not that these things won't serve the awakening process. They will, but it's time to cast off the old ways and awaken to the new.

The newness is ancient in that great teachers have always come upon this planet to teach the same lesson, but human beings want to deify the teacher instead of learning the lesson. It is now imperative that the lesson be learned, and the lesson has always been about love.

Each person has within them a ticking clock of awareness, and that clock is about to go off. It is the dawning of a new age, a new time is coming on this planet that has been anticipated for thousands of years. Alarms are going off, and there is no time left for hitting the snooze button. Many have already opened their eyes to this new day, but much must be done to assist everyone who is willing to wake up, if we are truly to honor all life. We must help each other in this process like psychic roosters crowing at the crack of dawn.

This does not mean that everyone will choose to awaken. Some are not yet ready for the responsibility of the new dimension opening on this beautiful planet. They are still caught in the fear cycle and the cycle of hatred that has been so pervasive for many years. Those who choose not to awaken will yet awaken at another time in another place. It is their choice and their destiny to choose the third-dimensional reality for another eon, and that is okay. Do not be alarmed that all are not ready. They will awaken in the perfect time for their own inner growth. It is not for us to judge the time frame for others.

For those reading this book, though, your appointed time is NOW or you wouldn't have been attracted to these words or to this understanding. This will be a wonderful day to awaken to, so don't be afraid of what is coming. In fact, that is your greatest challenge, to let go of the fear that is so prevalent.

There are specific ways to overcome your fears. You must release those things that maintain it. Let go of the steady diet of fear through the news on TV and in the newspapers. Can't you feel from your own daily experience that it ties you in knots to have a steady diet of fear—killings, war, rapes, murders, school shootings, all the things that make up your daily exposure to fear and destruction. Quit buying into the media hype that this is "what sells." You don't have to believe that anymore, nor do you need to choose values based on greed.

It's time to take responsibility for what you put into your minds. The mind is like a fabulous computer, and you are constantly programming fear by holding to the habit of daily negative exposure. Besides, it is a total distortion to think what is in the news represents reality. It's but a tiny fraction of what is going on in the world, and a small select group of individuals with a biased viewpoint make the selection each day as to what will be included. Imagine hiring cooks who, on a daily basis, poison your food. The media are poisoning minds on a daily basis with a steady diet of fear.

What do you think is the result of all this? Don't you feel it yourself after watching the news or have you numbed yourself to the effects of a constant diet of fear and hatred? The result is the belief that the world is rapidly going to hell, and there is no hope. The result is the desire for separation because you fear your fellow man. Has it ever occurred to you that it's much easier to control those who are fearful than those who are happy? I know you've heard the phrase, "divide and conquer." Throughout history, certain governments and the church have used fear as a means of control. That is because it really works.

If you are to be free, if you are to awaken to who you really are, if you are to summon the forces of light to be your allies, then you must find a way to bring yourself into a space of love, a place of peace. Light cannot penetrate the armor of hatred and fear unless you create the opening. That opening is love, which is absolutely the most powerful force within the universe. It is what holds the universe together, both figuratively and literally.

How to do this, you ask? Do what makes you feel good, what makes you feel connected to the divine energy that naturally flows within you. Maybe for you, it's a walk in a beautiful garden, maybe it's the feeling of love you feel toward your children as you watch them sleep, or the special connection you have with your pets. Just find the feeling in whatever way it works for you, then expand upon it. Create situations on a daily basis where you feel this sense of connection to the creative life force, whether it is prayer, meditation, Yoga, Tai Chi, mysticism, make your choice.

Take it from just where you found it and bring it out to others in your world. Share your positive feelings with those you love. You may find that by starting with what is easy, you can move toward what has been more difficult. Sometimes it's easier to start with strangers rather than your own family. Everyone can at least begin to smile more. That's a great start. Begin with what works for you, if you want to awaken at this time and ride the crest of the wave into a higher dimension. These changes must start within your own heart.

Truly, is that so difficult to understand? Isn't that what has been taught by all the great teachers? Isn't that what Jesus was saying. He didn't want to be deified or worshiped. He wanted to be emulated. He showed the way, but the path was muddied by lack of understanding and the unwillingness to follow in his footsteps. It was far easier to worship him and think of him as "the Savior" instead of being like him.

Two thousand years later, it is time to clear the path of debris. We must pick up the stones of hatred, clear out the branches of fear, and make the path clear for ourselves and others to follow. Once the path is clear, the journey will not be so difficult, and the destination will be delightful, even if there are a few diversions along the way as we learn to be good pathfinders. The whole point is to begin the journey one way or another. There is no time for further delay or folly.

The time is now. The alarm clock of destiny is being heard around the world, and the sleeping throngs are stumbling out of bed seeking what the new day will bring. It will bring hope, and it will bring love, and it will bring the dawning of a dimensional shift of proportions such as this world has never known. It will bring many changes as we move into this new, higher frequency. Don't fear the change, for it is just the process of labor as this beautiful world gives birth to something wonderful.

7

Changes...Changes ...Changes

We are in a time of great change. Government, education, financial institutions, farming—all these and more will undergo many changes. At first, some of these changes will seem negative. However, ultimately they will be for the good of all instead of just a few. There have been prophecies about earth changes for thousands of years, but it has also been said that a mass elevation of consciousness may alter these predictions. More than anything else, we need to view our planet with a different perspective.

We think that our world is so stable because we are used to walking upon the earth, and it stays put. We build our homes, our cities, our countries upon the earth knowing it is solid, that it takes eons of geological time to make any dramatic change. This is what we want to believe, but it is not true. We are building upon a living, breathing entity—Gaia or Terra or Earth, whatever you prefer. She is our Mother, as we learned through the Native Americans. In our arrogance, we thought it was a peculiarity of speech, a way primitive peoples believed. We were wrong.

Indigenous people know the earth is our Mother, because she nurtures and sustains us. She gives us everything to live a comfortable life—soil to grow our crops, air to breathe, water to drink. But look what we have done with her gifts. The Mother weeps for us because we are so unaware. Yet, we think of ourselves as being an advanced society, and the Native Americans as being primitive. It is the opposite. They lived in harmony with the Earth, in balance with nature. We must put away our pride and our swollen egos, and stop thinking of ourselves as so evolved. We are not. We must turn within to see the real source, which is God, or "Our Good," if that is easier for you. When we align with "Source," we will be in harmony with nature, as well.

I attended a conference at Mt. Shasta in May of 1995. The focus was on Ascension. At one point, all 300 people did a blessing and healing of Mother Earth. Spontaneously, some wept while others released negativity through breathing and toning, which is a harmonious sound voiced in unison. At the conclusion, we broke into vigorous applause and laughter. Earth was truly honored, and it was perfect because it just happened to be Mother's Day.

Our blessing was well received, but Mother is about to assert herself in a perfectly normal way, just as a mother might do with a naughty child, to set the child in the right direction. The earth changes everyone has talked about for so long are now a reality, especially the changes in weather. The Mother is trying to get our attention. Rather than thinking of the changes as being in the future, we need to open our eyes to the fact that they are already here. Just read the daily newspapers about worldwide disasters or listen to the evening news. There are earthquakes, tidal waves, floods, fires, and dramatic changes in the weather patterns.

What is happening now is just the beginning of what is to come. Rather than fear what is coming, it's time to prepare, a time to turn inward. This is all the Mother wants of us, an awakening awareness to what is truly important. Let me give you a clue about this. It isn't money, material goods, and high technology. It is love—love of self, love of each other, love of the Earth and all she provides. This is a time to return to a simple, cooperative existence, to grow our food and work together to create self-sustaining communities founded on positive values—love peace, and joyfulness.

We are being given an opportunity to learn once again the important lessons of life. Isn't that what a mother teaches, how to live a good life based on positive values? That is exactly the lesson of the earth changes, finding balance and harmony, turning away from greed and all that does not sustain us or the environment. The lesson is a simple one, and quite necessary.

Change is not a bad thing. It is good. It's exactly what will lead us back to values that are life-sustaining, not death-sustaining. We must learn to see with a different eye, an eye that is focused on love, not on fear. We will be tempted during these times of great change to choose fear instead. Let us be wise enough to be truly discerning.

Use this time of change as an opportunity to really open yourself to "Source," in whatever way is appropriate for you. The term I prefer, personally, is "The Creative Life Force." For me, that says it all. Regardless of what you call it, as you tune into this inner awareness, it will guide you to exactly where you need to be. I mean that in a very literal sense. I tried unsuccessfully for years to get my family to move from the West Coast until I finally realized that everyone will be exactly where they need to be to experience whatever lessons they need to learn. My mother finally said in exasperation, "If the earthquake doesn't kill me, the move would." We can be so tempted to think we know what is best for someone else, but they must find their own truth, and we must learn to release them to their fate. Besides, there is no death in the way we think of it. It is but a very thin veil that separates us from those who pass over. An excellent book about this is *We Don't Die: A Skeptic's Discovery of Life After Death*, by Sandra Champlain and Dr. Bernie Siegel.

We need to face what is ahead, not only with courage but with a sense of adventure. It's time to release so much of what we thought important, what we thought was real. Frequently, the possessions we think we own become our masters, and we are their slaves. Let go and move on. Release and see how much lighter, how much freer you feel, if you do it with the right attitude because attitude is everything. We choose whether to experience this time of change as an opportunity or as a burden. That is our choice. We cannot always choose the circumstances surrounding us, but we always have a choice about how we will respond. That is our true power, the choice to choose love, peace, harmony, cooperation, or the opposite.

We can learn during these times to live in harmony with the land and with each other. That is the lesson of the Native Americans, and what they can teach us if we open ourselves to their knowledge. We are in a time of great lessons and a time of great personal empowerment. We need to be willing to turn away from the old and familiar to embrace the new that is coming into existence. It's going to come anyway. We might as well learn to open our hearts and minds to this wonderful new time coming upon us.

Some of the more positive changes will be great breakthroughs in health and healing. I think the medicine of the future will be light, sound, and color, which are all based on frequencies. I already have an extraordinary device invented by Brian David Anderson known as the Multi-Tranz. It's a frequency generator set at the frequency for oxygen, and it alters the molecular structure of all fluids, enhancing the taste. It also has a healing effect on the human body which is primarily water.

Another positive change taking place is that people are becoming more openly intuitive. This will especially be a wonderful boost for men, given that women have tended to be more gifted in this way. It will help balance the male-female energies, and allow us an opportunity to learn some new, quite interesting lessons.

8

LESSONS HAPPEN

WE NEED TO realize that we are here on this planet to do more than live a mundane life. We are here to serve others, and we are here to learn. That's it in a nutshell, pure and simple.

Lessons come in all sizes and shapes. Sometimes they arise from what appear to be catastrophic circumstances, other times the lessons are quite simple. If we don't learn the lesson the first time around, we frequently are doomed to relive the lesson on an ever-expanding basis. That is how destructive patterns get established in our lives, by not learning the lesson the first time around. "Here I go again," is what we frequently may feel once one of these patterns gets established. Repetitive patterns are always a clue to look deeper within for the cause.

Patterns are not established just in this lifetime. They are frequently holdovers from previous lives, lessons that were not learned in the past coming up again, offering another opportunity to get it right this time. We are given many opportunities to "get it right," which is greatly to our benefit. Lessons are not to be feared. They are our friends, our opportunity for growth. It's actually a wonderful system, like special private schools where each child is educated on an individual basis.

The big group lesson in the United States centers on greed. It is part of the lesson of the capitalist system, which would work so well if only it was used along with a sense of wanting only good for all concerned, a win-win situation. Greed continues instead to create a win-lose scenario. This will never work, as far as universal law is concerned. Pope Francis had a lot to say about this when he visited the United States in 2015. He is a good teacher in that regard.

Jesus taught universal law by teaching love. It is what the Golden Rule is all about: "Do unto others as you would have them do unto you." Another version of the same concept is karma, or the law of cause and effect. Stated simply, "What goes around, comes around."

Why can't we see how simple it is? Instead, we continue to fall back into a kindergarten mentality and focus on "me" and "mine" instead of "us" and "ours." We are here to serve others, not to be islands unto ourselves; but in serving others with loving intentions, we actually serve ourselves. Remember, "what goes around, comes around." This is it in its most basic form—giving and receiving love. Giving to others is actually quite pleasurable.

One of the greatest problems is the lack of self-love. If self-love was more prevalent, there would be something to give others. We are frequently raised in homes where love is not modeled on any level whatever. Instead, physical, emotional, and sexual abuse are at an all-time high—the result of moral and spiritual decay accompanied by the stress of a highly technological society which often treats people as expendable. Yet, we must learn love of self to truly love others.

So, where to begin? Begin with finding yourself. Recognize who you are. You are a spiritual being acting out a human lifetime. Go back to your roots, back to the Life Force in whatever way feels good to you. Maybe you need to return to the church of your youth. Just go sometime when no one else is there. Sit in the chapel or the sanctuary, look at the beauty surrounding you, maybe a ray of sunshine coming through a stained-glass window. Recapture the feelings, if you ever had them, of being in the presence of God. Bow your head, close your eyes, pray in whatever way feels right for you. Seek guidance and help to awaken to who you really are, to awaken to the love and light pouring forth from God. It is a constant. It is always there for you.

Maybe for you, church is the last place you will feel this connection. If that is the case, go to somewhere beautiful in nature. Even in cities, there are parks where you can feel the grass or experience the trees. If it's cold out, find an indoor setting, possibly a botanical garden or even a lovely atrium in a beautiful, modern building. Just find a place to sit quietly to reflect on who you really are—a divine spark of life. The one most important part of this internal process, whether you call it prayer, meditation, or reflection, is to go within and ask for assistance. Most people forget to ask for help, not recognizing that it is always there for them.

You might want to focus on God or on Jesus, or maybe you prefer to think of angels or your guides. The way you view assistance coming is not as important as the need to ask. "Seek, and you shall find." "Ask, and you shall receive." These are not idle words or Biblical poetry. We must do the asking because this is part of our spiritual journey, to get to the place of realization that we are not alone, and to know we may call on powerful forces to assist us in all we do.

We must manifest a willingness to move on with our lives. In the last chapter we discussed the great changes that are upon us. The changes are here now, not just coming in the future, and they are here whether you like it or not. The sooner we learn to adapt and to "go with the flow" instead of resisting, the easier we make it on ourselves. In the same way, learning to view all that happens to us as an opportunity to learn a lesson makes life easier. Just say to yourself, "I wonder what I'm supposed to learn from this." The following quote is the daily message from the *Daily Word* for September 29, 2015:

> "I gracefully move through life's transitions. As colder days approach, trees shed their leaves and animals prepare for hibernation. They instinctively move through the seasons. In contrast, humans are prone to resisting change even though we know that it is an essential part of growth. I may notice myself worrying or fighting change. Then I remind myself I am able to prepare and move through any change I encounter."

I envision myself shedding old beliefs and ways of being just as a tree releases leaves. Like the hibernating animals, I prepare my mind and body for a time of quiet and reflection. I see divine order in the leaves reappearing each spring. My life also follows a pattern. I emerge from each season stronger, wiser, and more loving.

"For everything there is a season, and a time for every matter under heaven."—Ecclesiastes 3:1

There is an old, much-used saying, "Whatever you resist, persists." Whatever you resist becomes one of those frequently repeated patterns until you learn the lesson. We need to look at these times as the greatest opportunity to learn that has ever been offered to this planet. Some will learn what they need to learn, and some will not. Some will go into a higher dimensional reality, and some will not. The lesson is actually quite easy, make the choice of love rather than the choice of fear.

It is an easy choice between two specific feelings and attitudes. More difficult is the willingness to let go of all other needs and desires. We have a tendency to complicate life by holding on to "our stuff," both literally and figuratively, so this is now our challenge. It will also be our blessing. We truly need to learn to release on so many levels.

9

Learning to Let Go

LIFE IS WONDERFULLY exciting, from the right perspective. It challenges us to grow, to learn constantly to let go of the past so we can move into the future unfettered. What happens, though, for most people, is an unwillingness to release. We are afraid to lose what we have because of the unknown lying before us.

Creating something new is so much easier if you just learn to release the old. This is true in simple ways, such as giving away those clothes you are no longer wearing to create space for new clothes. It always surprises me when I see a woman's closet filled to the brim with clothes that probably go back for decades. What is the point? Oftentimes the clothes even have negative reminders, like having been a size seven in the past when she's now a size fourteen. I sometimes wonder if she sees the analogy of "holding onto weight" in the same way as she is holding onto the clothes from the past, but I never say anything unless it comes out in a therapist-client relationship where it's my function to teach.

Accumulation happens on all levels. It happens with things. It happens with toxic build-up in our bodies, and the inability to eliminate properly. It happens with old ideas, old concepts, old feelings associated with past trauma. It happens in all areas of our lives.

Why are we such pack rats? Why don't we see how easy the solution is, to just learn to release? The problem is fear—

fear that there may not be something to replace the old. In relationships, it's the fear of being alone. Frequently, with negative feelings or judgments from the past, it is the unwillingness to forgive, the result of not recognizing that holding onto these feelings and thoughts is much more damaging than the original offense. This is one of the greatest accumulations of toxicity in the body, holding onto these feelings—choosing, essentially, to be a victim.

Forgiveness is life's greatest healer, a tool more useful than any other to release the past with grace. I tell my clients to not think of it as being a priest absolving someone of their sins. It's not about going to confession or a religious ritual. It's about releasing the negative thoughts and images that bind one to the past in hurtful ways. When we carry with us all these judgments of perceived wrongdoings, those feelings, thoughts, and images are truly hurting us. Lack of forgiveness is the real source of disease (dis-ease) in our world. As I said earlier in Chapter Two, we must learn to forgive if we truly desire happiness. We also must learn to forgive if we want to let go of the past to create our future in a more positive way.

Forgiveness is a great gift. Not only does it release you, but it releases the other person you have held in contempt in your mind. If necessary, start with the small judgments, like forgiving the person who cut you off on your way to work or the person who grabbed your seat on the subway. Work backward from there, all the way back to the "biggies," like your ex-spouse, your former boyfriend or girlfriend, your kids, and the really big one for many people, your parents. Don't forget to forgive yourself in the process. That is an absolute necessity.

This is not an exercise that only takes an hour or two. It takes a lifetime. You need to be in a state of constant forgiveness. It is a wonderful idea from a health standpoint to be working at the same time with a body therapist to release the physical trauma stored in the cells, the "cellular memory," and to work with a colonic therapist to release the "shit" stored in the body. Combining all levels of release—the spiritual, mental, and physical—will greatly accelerate your growth process and give you a tremendous sense of freedom, beyond anything you have ever experienced.

What is the effect on the world when you choose to let go? It is a sense of freedom and release on a grander scale. We are all linked through consciousness. If just once, even only for a few minutes, everyone came together in thinking a loving thought, feeling it within their being, it would totally transform the planet. I have often wondered in the middle of making love what the effect would be if all the lovers on the planet had an orgasm at the same time. It would certainly be a different version, a more exciting and healing version of the Big Bang theory of creation!

10

Coming Together

Coming together in love, in the emotional, physical, and sexual sense, is a big deal. The pursuit of a perfect mate occupies a great deal of time, both in thought and deed, for the majority of people. If we put so much time into it, why do the final results often seem so unsatisfying? Why is the divorce rate so extraordinarily high?

One of the reasons is that most people are looking for someone to love them, but they have never learned to love—either themselves or others. We have very poor cultural role models when it comes to loving. Can you think of many television show couples or celebrity relationships you would want to emulate? Much of what we see all around us is the exact opposite, especially on soap operas. We frequently don't have good role models at home, either. There are only a lucky few who would say, "I want a relationship just like Mom and Dad's."

Why are we so screwed up when it comes to love? One reason is we equate love and sex in this culture. These are two completely different things. It is very nice when you have both within one relationship, but they are not equated. Sometimes when a person says, "I am in love," they really mean, "I am in lust," and I'm not saying this to make a moral judgment. Lust is something most people feel at one time or another, and it can certainly be a wonderful opportunity to learn important lessons, but getting it confused with love will definitely lead to problems.

There is another problem related to the way we view romantic love. We expect bells to go off in our heads when Mr. or Ms. Wonderful shows up. We want to feel like we are walking on air for awhile. No wonder the decisions about mates are frequently ill-made. We aren't even grounded at the time we make them.

Other times, anyone who indicates any interest at all is seen as a potential mate, simply because it beats being alone. What does that say about a person's self-esteem? Frequently, people who come from abusive backgrounds manage to choose abusive mates to perpetuate the pattern of abuse because they think and feel that's all they deserve.

How do we learn to make healthy decisions about who to love in a male-female relationship? The same question holds true for male-male or female-female relationships, if a person is gay. There are a lot of tumultuous gay relationships, too, especially in a society that is so homophobic. Developing a positive sense of self-esteem is almost impossible for a young gay person. If the straight role models are few and far between, the gay role models are even more hidden. However, now that gay marriage is becoming legal in more and more states, there are many openly gay couples. This is a good thing. We definitely need more love in the world.

We must first love ourselves if we are to love another successfully. I'm sure that phrase seems trite to some, but the fact is it is absolute truth with a capital "T." The ideal way to learn this is to be raised in a loving home with parents who are warm and encouraging, parents who purposely take actions and use words that contribute to a child's self-esteem. Since many individuals did not experience such an environment, they must create one on their own to learn how to love.

This can be done with a warm and loving therapist or with a variety of self-help groups, but not the ones that only focus on problems. All that does is reinforce problems, not solutions. There are many sources for growth in self-awareness, running the gamut from secular to spiritual. Up until now, though, there have been many more females willing to engage in this type of growth than males. It is now time for the males to wake up, and many will. The more recent phenomena of male bonding groups is part of that process.

The energy of the planet is shifting now back toward the feminine, and that side within men is awakening. This is a wonderful time to be here on Earth because we are in the process of coming back toward balance after being out of balance for so long. It is time to put an end to the "war of the sexes." It is time to form harmonious relationships with a balance of emotional and rational perceptions of reality, as we come together in sensitivity and cooperation.

From a political standpoint, we must put aside the male dominance, competition, and the need to be right. The time for all that is over. It would be nice to awaken tomorrow and find that all this was a thing of the past, but as long as we're still into third-dimensionality, it will be a process of release rather than an overnight occurrence. For those, though, who do make the shift to a higher dimension, that is the kind of world they will experience. What a fabulous thing that will be.

Since most of us aren't to that point yet, what can be done within personal relationships to move in that direction? Some of the best material that helped me in this process was *A Course in Miracles*, an extraordinary teaching that emerged in the mid-70s. Back then you learned about it through word-of-mouth among spiritual seekers. I first bought the three books as a self-study course while traveling down the California coast through Big Sur. There were no organized groups at the time. You just went through the material on your own. However, it grew to a whole movement with study groups, additional books, and even television programs.

Some people had difficulty with the traditional Christian language, although the manuscript was written by an atheistic Jewish woman. I was still somewhat into my religious rebellion at the time, so I had difficulty with the terminology, but I turned God into "good" and Jesus into "Christ Consciousness." By doing this, I was able to learn a whole different perception, one that at the time felt like a foreign language. It did concern me that *A Course in Miracles* became an institution unto itself and was treated like a religion rather than a spiritual teaching. However, it is still a wonderful source for learning forgiveness and nonjudgmental thinking.

Another positive source for those who wanted to move into a more advanced focus on light as the energy of love on this planet was the Mahatma teachings. The book is still available as *Mahatma I and II*, by Brian Grattan, now deceased. It was channeled through Brian and led to gatherings throughout Canada and the United States. By utilizing the Mahatma energy, a person could break down the destructive patterns that exist on the physical, emotional, and spiritual levels. This was done in groups or as individuals and did not require the presence of Brian.

Another source that is more recent is Gaia Television through the Internet. It has multiple programs on spirituality, Yoga, and even "Cosmic Disclosure," which I mentioned in chapters 4 and 5. I highly recommend this programming.

As a person moves into his or her teaching of choice, whether it is psychotherapy, a church teaching, *A Course in Miracles*, the Mahatma energy, Gaia Television, or any other path toward growth and enlightenment, he or she will meet others along the path, as well. This is a far greater and more positive pool to draw from for a potential mate than the local singles bar or computer dating. "Like attracts like" at the energy level, so if you want to attract someone wonderful, spend more time becoming wonderful yourself. That brings us full circle to the need for self-love in order to love another effectively.

11

Playful Passion

W E ARE IN love with romance in this country—in love with the idea of romance. It peeks out at us in advertisements and through the multitude of television programs, the Internet, movies, books, and in many other more subtle ways. Unfortunately, romance and love are two different things, just as sex and love are different.

We want our men to be romantic, but what does that mean? It usually means we want them to send flowers, to bring us gifts, to choose romantic cards for us. We want them to be sensitive. We want them to take us to places with a romantic atmosphere. We want them to hold our hands, to just cuddle sometimes rather than assume that every touch is sexual in nature.

What's wrong with that, you say? Absolutely nothing. Believe me, I'm all for the above and more. In fact for a few years I was one of the "Romance Doctors" along with Stephen Mason. We answered questions as "he says" and "she says" in a column for a popular singles newspaper, and did our *schtick* on the radio and for public appearances. I love romance and I love romantic men.

However, I also recognize romance as the frosting on the cake, not the real substance. If a relationship is founded on romance or on "being in lust," it truly is on a shaky foundation that is likely to crumble. Our whole way of dating is based on physical attraction and sex appeal, which is constantly reinforced by the media. Sexual attraction is supposed to lead to romance, and romance is supposed to lead to marriage, and all this is supposed to equal love. The only problem is that it doesn't. It equals an illusion of love.

As I said before, I love romance, and I love sex, too. I am not a religious curmudgeon saying we should give this all up. Life would be very dull indeed without playful passion, but it isn't what successful relationships are based on for the long haul. The true foundation must be love.

We must not only learn to love ourselves in order to love others, we also must learn to be effective communicators in and out of bed. When I say effective communicators, I'm not just talking about expressing words and feelings. I'm talking about learning to do it with love, with kindness, learning to do it in a way that will heal and not hurt.

It saddens me when I hear the way men and women communicate. So many times it's in a hurtful style, even when it is supposedly "just kidding." The communication is often a put-down or a power play. When you listen to men and women talking either to each other, or about the opposite sex, what do you frequently hear? Certainly, not words of love, harmony, and peace. The war of the sexes is alive and well, but it's time for a truce which needs to lead to lasting peace.

There is no reason to have to constantly hurt another's self-esteem or confidence, even when you break up and go your separate ways. The real lesson is to learn to release in love, and want for that other person to find happiness. What goes around, comes around, and what you put out is ultimately what you get back. Learn to speak words that are loving and kind, to your romantic partner and to all others, as well.

This is especially true in bed. A person has a very different reaction to, "I love it when you touch me gently, with long, slow strokes," than to, "You never touch me right!" You can teach your sexual partner to be more sensitive to your needs, but it doesn't work if your words are judgmental or harsh. It only pushes people away or gets defenses up so they come back at you in an equally harsh, judgmental manner.

One of the most important lessons I taught when doing sex therapy was to "lighten up." Sex is supposed to be adult play; it's supposed to be fun. I love the whole concept of "playful passion," because playful sexuality is so much more healing to the relationship. Men and women, sexual partners as a whole, straight or gay, need to bring laughter into the bedroom, not a sense of competition. There's more than enough competitiveness in all other aspects of our lives, especially in this culture.

I love the idea of creating an adult toy chest in the bedroom. Maybe it contains certain costumes you have fun with in bed. Hopefully, it has many sensual delights such as special oils for massage, or powder to make the skin feel silky smooth. One of the easiest means of creating a sensual atmosphere is to always use a favorite scent that is only used when in a romantic mood—perfume, cologne, incense, or whatever appeals to both of you. The olfactory sense is very easily conditioned, so use it to work for you in a pleasurable way.

Another playful way of being together sexually is letting each of you choose a particular sexual fantasy to act out together. I know couples who like to play "first date" or who go somewhere to be "picked up" by their partners. Sometimes they end up at home or they may borrow a friend's apartment for a rendezvous or stay at a romantic hotel or inn. There are so many ways to play together. Remember how as kids it was so easy to get into make-believe situations and roles? Allow the kid in you to re-emerge. It can add spice to a loving relationship and make it a lot more fun.

There are many ways for touch to become more central to a relationship, too. This is a very touch deprived culture, partly because all touching is sexualized. Legitimate massage therapists frequently go through so much regulation in order to practice because of the societal fear that if it's pleasurable, it must be sexual. It could mean so much to elderly people, and to children, too, if massage became a routine practice in nursing homes and daycare centers. What a tremendous comfort that would be, a way to greatly soothe an elderly person's loneliness or to calm a child's overabundance of energy. Unfortunately, we have become a society looking for signs of sexual abuse in every touch. This perceptual distortion has led to even greater touch phobia in an already uptight culture.

For a couple, though, there is more freedom to enjoy touch which may or may not lead to sex. Just deciding on a regular basis to let one or the other be the receiver without the need to respond is a blessing. Stroking someone while they are drifting off to sleep is such a gift and such a sensual experience, but it needs to be agreed ahead of time if this will be one of those nights where the receiver can fall asleep or if this will be a time where the touch is the beginning of foreplay and needs to be reciprocal. It's not appropriate for one or the other to always be the receiver and to never reciprocate or to always fall asleep and never become aroused. Both partners must learn to give and to receive if the relationship is truly based on love. Frequently, one or the other is usually the giver, but both roles are necessary in a balanced relationship.

What about monogamy? Is it a necessity for a truly loving relationship? For most people, yes, but not for everyone. Some people have learned that love is not limited to only one person. Love doesn't get "used up" if you give it away. Instead, the more love you give, the more love there is to give. It just keeps increasing, like priming the pump, if you are truly in a space of unconditional love. The problem for most people, though, is they feel too insecure to share a partner with anyone else, and the idea brings up all kinds of fears leading to jealousy and possessiveness. Unless both partners have reached a very advanced level of unconditional love, monogamy is probably an easier base on which to form a relationship founded in trust. What many do is "serial monogamy," in that we move on from one partner at a time to another partner, once the previous relationship is completed.

A relationship that lasts forever is not a perfect measure of success. That was the idea many of our parents or grandparents bought into, but it did not necessarily produce a satisfying relationship that was nurturing. The important qualities are respect, trust, commitment to be there for each other and, hopefully, a willingness to evolve toward unconditional love. Too many times, a relationship becomes the exact opposite. Our partner is the least likely to support or respect our feelings or desires. If that's the case, it's time for a significant evaluation of why you are staying in an abusive or non-supportive relationship. If you truly love and honor yourself, you don't stay in a situation where you are surrounded constantly by negativity. Finding a therapist or attending a couple's workshop can significantly revamp a failing relationship. Other times, it is an absolute necessity to learn to let go, to release the relationship; but do it in a loving, healing way.

Taking your relationship or your partner for granted is a major error, yet almost everyone does this at one time or another. As soon as that starts to happen, you need to confront the problem and decide together not to let it continue to the point of feeling detached from each other. This is a perfect time to take a weekend away together, to rekindle the romance and feelings of connection. Be willing to give and take, so that sometimes you may do something he loves, like a weekend in the woods; and maybe another time do what she loves, possibly go somewhere to dance the night away.

Learning to respect and honor the needs of your partner is something that should have been learned at home by watching your parents. However, that is frequently not where it's learned anymore, and sometimes it's never learned. The learning process is greatly assisted, though, when you mentally and emotionally understand how those early parental relationships are affecting your present situation. Look at your history, not with the intention to blame parents for present shortcomings, but with an understanding that leads to wisdom and the ability to change what didn't work in the past.

12

Kids, Parents, and Other Strangers

There is often a barrier between those who should be closest, those within our own families. A person may have a lovely, open personality on the job, then come home and be a perfect stranger at home, or even worse, a tyrant. Why is that? Why do we hurt those closest to us, those we supposedly love?

There are millions of people walking around every day who feel abused, abused at work or at home. Sometimes, it's true in a very literal sense; but at other times, it comes from being beaten down by the everyday stresses encountered in our society. A person may awaken to the morning news on television, which is like tuning into the daily homicide report. Then they may gulp down coffee and grab a donut, their first hit of caffeine and sugar for the day. Commuting might mean rush hour on the subway or on a busy freeway with delays, increasing their blood pressure because of the fear of being late to a job they hate anyway. At work, there may be deadlines or personality clashes to deal with.

The on-the-job meals are frequently more sugar or fat, gulped down rapidly because of the need to run a quick errand. All of this might even be accompanied by cigarettes—the nicotine hit, or maybe even a cocktail at lunch. Then there is the rushed trip home or the late night at the office. When they finally walk into their home, they may feel exhausted.

At this point, men often sit down in front of the television for the less-than-positive evening news, while women don't even get that break, because they have to deal with kids or dinner or both. After dinner, there's time for more television, typically cynical humor or lots of violence or maybe some violent computer games. This is frequently accompanied by more alcohol consumption and/or junk food. Right before bedtime, there's one more chance to get blasted with the horrors of the day by watching the late-night news, before drifting off to a fitful sleep.

I just described a typical American lifestyle. How does it sound? Does it sound healthy? Is there much satisfaction or peace of mind? I think not.

How can people possibly relate to each other in a positive way when they subject themselves to that kind of lifestyle? It reminds me of the rat studies in Psychology 101, in which overcrowded rats become aggressive or even cannibalistic. Although, most city dwellers aren't eating each other literally, at a figurative level they are certainly being eaten up by stress. No wonder the big American disease is cancer. We've created a way to die by being eaten up at the cellular level, and it certainly is a reflection of a disturbed society and lifestyle—at an emotional, spiritual, and environmental level.

If we are going to have positive relationships at home and elsewhere, it is imperative to "de-stress" in the ways we can control. I learned way back in the mid-70s to turn off the television news and not listen to "noise" on my car radio on the way to work. At the time, I was a single mom with two kids going to graduate school at the University of Washington. I have continued in that manner in that I have now not had regular television for at least eleven years. I do not have cable or Direct TV. Instead, I use my large, flat screen TV to watch DVD's, movies or television series of my choice without commercials. More recently, I have added Netflix because my adult daughter came to live with me and she set it up. I get enough of the news on the Internet and in the daily newspaper, probably more than enough.

I have chosen different lifestyles over the last many years based on my work and where I was living. I moved to Las Vegas in 1992, and never would have thought in the past that I would eventually live there. However, since then I have lived in many places, all within Nevada. I moved to Pahrump, a small town west of Las Vegas, in 2004, and have lived here since then—first on a 6½-acre ranch and now in a lovely small home in a quiet, senior community. I retired as a psychologist in 2014, and presently have more freedom to write and do other things. On the ranch, for a time, I had 13 goats—a wonderful animal that literally jumps for joy, especially when young.

Now, I'm sure that some of you are saying, "Yeah, but you don't have kids to contend with or a husband at home waiting to be fed." That is true, at present. However, I raised two kids almost completely on my own as a single mom while going through ten years of college. I have had two marriages—one when I was very young where I actually had the experience of being a housewife for several years while my kids were little. The other marriage was after the kids were grown. He was a professor, and we were two busy professionals living and loving together. Much later I was with a partner for six years and was planning to get married again on 10/10/10, but he unexpectedly died on 3/16/10. These relationships gave me the opportunity to live very different lifestyles with their accompanying satisfaction and stresses. Believe me, I have done my time when it comes to lifestyle stress, in every sense of the word. That's exactly why I have chosen to live differently now. I consciously and purposefully eliminate or greatly decrease my everyday stress by choosing to live a positive, healthy life. Presently, I practice Spring Forest Qigong and also do water aerobics three time a week, but Tai Chi and Yoga are also helpful practices.

When you choose to live a healthy lifestyle, you can have so much more to give emotionally and in every other way to those you love the most, and to yourself. You might even have some energy left over after a busy day to play with the kids or to make love to your spouse or lover. Even if you begin only gradually to let go of some of the greatest stressors and time-wasters (like television and computer games), I guarantee you, you will begin to feel lighter and more energized. This is especially true if you combine this with positive, healthy nutrition.

Another area, though, that must be cleared to have positive relations with family is your own emotional scars from your upbringing. You must bring enough self-awareness to your relationships to not always be acting out destructive patterns from your past. It is quite common for people to blame their parents for their shortcomings. Maybe they were abused or neglected, maybe they were abandoned either physically or emotionally, maybe they were not provided for financially.

It's time, once and for all, for all of us to put aside being victims—victims of our parents or in any other way we might buy into that concept. At a deep level—let's use the term "soul" since it is more understood and accepted in this culture—at the soul level you have chosen the circumstances of your birth, your parents, and in general, the challenges you will experience in life. This is your way of choosing the exact lessons you need to learn in this particular incarnation. Yet, we are eternal beings. We incarnate in each lifetime in specific relationships with other souls we have been involved with previously. This culture has been greatly retarded in its spiritual growth by not understanding this simple truth.

Your choice of parents may be those souls who were once your children in a previous incarnation, or maybe your spouse, or your siblings. These are the specific souls you have unfinished business with, which is why you connect again, to complete the lessons that were unlearned, to balance a wrong from the past, or to bless a previous right. The understanding of reincarnation was there during the lifetime of Jesus and is alluded to several times in the Bible. Many more reincarnation references were part of the original Bible, but they were removed in 553 A.D. at the Fifth Ecumenical Congress of Constantinople so that the church could exert greater control over the populous. If someone thought, "I'll get it right next lifetime," he might not be as easy to manipulate this time around.

Given that we choose our parents, and our kids choose us, it creates a whole new understanding of what that relationship is about. It is about learning unconditional love. Once again, it's very simple, when one asks a question about relationships, frequently the answer is "learn to love more, learn to forgive, learn to release in love," or something on that theme. If you were abused by your parents, or if you have been less than loving toward your children, it is time to re-evaluate that whole scenario in terms of forgiveness to reconnect in a loving way, and to move on. Sometimes this has to be done completely at the mental level because parents may be deceased or displaced. Even at the mental level, learning to forgive parents, children, spouses, and yourself gives you a tremendous boost forward in consciousness; and that is the ultimate goal, your own personal growth.

There is nothing too awful to be forgiven. The forgiveness is your release from the situation. As long as you are still fighting a situation, even if it is just in your mind, you are not free from it. Forgiveness is your ticket to freedom and peace of mind. It is your means of getting on track to do your personal work in this world.

Many people are on a quest to answer one question: "What did I come here to do?" Most likely, it is right there all around you. You came to learn to love and to learn to forgive. When you do it at the most basic level, around the issues of parenthood—your parents and your kids—the next level of your growth will become obvious, and you will be able to move on with love, grace, and wisdom to discover your "real work." You may even discover that your real job is much different than what you are presently doing. We have many more options than most of us realize.

13

Jobs Are Optional

THERE ARE MILLIONS of people every day in this country commuting to jobs they hate. No wonder there is so much dissatisfaction. No wonder the socially accepted drugs such as sugar, caffeine, nicotine, and alcohol are used and abused so widely. No wonder street drugs are so prevalent, and the biggest addictions of all in this culture are even abused by children—cell phones, television, and the Internet. Looking at our society with its horribly destructive lifestyles gives us a peek at the encroaching social decay and decline well on its way. Where is all this leading to, and what can be done?

Just as each of us must turn inward to seek the light of love and understanding, so too must businesses and major employers do the same. If the business is not serving its customers and its employees, it must be reworked. In the past, I worked in a practice where we did a lot of work with people injured on the job, people who were in the process of rehabilitation to return to work. I saw firsthand the abuses of some employers, the (SIIS) State Industrial Insurance System, doctors, and sometimes the employees themselves; but it is much more often the system itself in workman's compensation that is failing to serve, rather than the injured workers abusing the system.

All this must change. We are coming into a time on this planet where the old ways of authoritarianism, competition, and aggression—the dominant force within the male energy system—will no longer work. The energy is shifting back to the feminine force, and it is ultimately becoming more balanced. The old will begin to fall away in all societal systems as the new begins to evolve, and the new approaches will be based on cooperation, service to others, peace and harmony. That's what will work now. The sooner individuals and the corporate world begin to understand and implement that, the better it will be for all of us.

If you are one of those people in a job you hate or in a business that cares nothing for your personal welfare, it is time to re-evaluate your situation, time to look at all your options. We all have many more options than we allow ourselves to see, and this is the time to pull back the curtains to see clearly what is out there.

Many more people will begin to choose the option of working for themselves, being their own boss. It's a great time for entrepreneurs, and many of the most successful businesses will in some way cater to the basics—food, water, energy-efficient dwellings in small communities, clothing, alternative energy sources, alternative health products, and creative inventions. It is a time where communication will be valued—the kind of communication systems that will allow families to move out of the cities and back into safer, more secure small towns. There are already many people developing mail order businesses and using the Internet in a way that makes location more flexible. They can live in a beautiful, natural setting and operate a successful business at the same time.

We are returning to a time where more simple values will be appreciated once again. It is the present desire for so many "things," the rampant materialism which is reinforced on all sides through the media and mass consumerism, that becomes the oppressor. Has it ever occurred to you that you have become a slave to your possessions? You work at a job you hate just to have all the so-called goodies in your life—the car, the house, the boat, the expensive clothes, along with all your other possessions. Or maybe you're just getting by. Does this lifestyle really bring you satisfaction? Are you truly happy? The answer can't possibly be "yes" on a mass basis because all we need to do is look around us to see that our society is not a reflection of great joy, but quite the opposite.

What can you do personally to change this? What are your personal options? Everyone needs to find that answer for themselves, but I would suggest you begin to re-evaluate your talents, what you like to do, what ways you might best be of service to others. What are those things that really do make you happy? How do you like to spend your time? Are there ways you can turn your hobbies into businesses? Are there ways for you to make money doing what you love? You must be thoughtful and creative with this. Take your time in considering your talents. The first step is to allow the idea itself, the desire for change, to flow into your consciousness. It might begin with a question to yourself, "Is this all there is—getting up, going to work, going home, going to bed, then starting the whole thing over again? There must be more to life."

The first step is always to go within, to begin to ask yourself those questions that will lead to answers and options. Start really exploring all this, and do it with gusto and humor. It doesn't have to be serious drudgery. A bookstore or Amazon.com are great resources. There are magazines on almost every hobby and topic you can think of. That's a start. Get some magazines or look up magazines on the Internet that may give you ideas you want to pursue. As you narrow it down, find appropriate books to gain a greater awareness of your chosen area of interest.

Don't limit yourself in the beginning of your search, be expansive and make it fun. Begin to think about those places you might prefer to live. Are you ready for a smaller town? Do you prefer another part of the country? Maybe you have relatives who live in a completely different environment who might assist you in some way to make a move. Contact the local chamber of commerce once you narrow it down. That's a perfect way to really learn about a new community. Subscribe to the local newspaper. This is what I have always done when I wanted to move to a new location. It's a wonderful way to spur your imagination.

When I left my large, three-office practice back east, I decided not to practice psychology for a period of time. I wanted to explore other options, but most of all I wanted a break from the intensity of the lifestyle I was leaving. I had been traveling back and forth between three offices, seeing many clients, doing the administrative work required in a private practice, doing television and radio. I was ready for a change. I also knew at an inner level there was important work for me to do that would never happen in that setting.

I turned my offices over to my associates, sold almost everything I owned, and loaded what was left into a small trailer, which I pulled across country with my little red and black Nissan Pulsar. I had my two cats as my travel companions. We took off for the West Coast on a quest for our future, and moved onto a 42-foot powerboat with my son on reaching Southern California. I had the forecabin and loved the gentle rocking at night and the creaking of the lines that secured the boat to the dock. The cats learned to come and go on their own, although my oldest one, Mu Shu, would sometimes get on the wrong dock. He would go down the distance to where the boat should have been, then begin to yowl when he didn't find it. Friendly neighbors would usually return him promptly to the correct dock.

We lived on the boat for three months—about as long as I felt my son could handle three intruders, although he was always more than gracious. That was the first phase of my journey into a new life, a journey that ultimately took me to Las Vegas via Sedona, Arizona, first. I thought this was just a stopover, but I have now been in Nevada for twenty-four years. What a surprise. As usual, though, I have lived in many different locations here—Las Vegas, Mt. Charleston, Reno, Las Vegas again, Boulder City, and now Pahrump where I have been for over twelve years.

We all have the option and opportunity to change our lives, even if we choose to do it in a more gradual manner. We must follow our passion and joy to our ultimate destiny. If you feel no passion or joy, then the first step is to discover it; and it always comes by connecting to the life force. It is really an awakening to the fact that you are already one with the life force, and that never changes.

Choose to live your life in a way that serves others, and you will more rapidly recognize your oneness with the life force. Even if your job is not directly a service-oriented job, begin to see the way it serves you. You will find the greatest benefit by first finding joy in your present work environment, even if has been a job that you previously hated. This is an exercise in changing your present way of viewing things, an opportunity to practice a more positive attitude.

Begin to recognize that it serves you by giving you a paycheck, then begin to look for all the good, even if at first it is hard to find. Maybe you work in a nice setting, and you can appreciate that. If not, maybe you can be appreciative of one or more of your coworkers. Begin to see them as people just like you, people who are there to support themselves and/or their families, sacrificing their time in an exchange for money. Begin to see all your coworkers, even your boss, as children of God. When you are able to bring some light of gratitude into your present work situation, no matter what the circumstances are, you will more rapidly be preparing yourself to move on to other options, if that's what you want. I am practicing this myself so I can move on from being a psychologist to a full-time writer.

Gratitude is exceptionally important in all that we do. The difference between a person who lives life graciously and one who lives under a cloud of darkness is frequently the ability to be thankful. We may not always be able to control the circumstances of our lives, but we do have control over our reaction. Our reaction is based on our perception of the circumstances so all we need to do is work on the way we view things.

Life gives us so much to be thankful for. As more people begin to share in this understanding, they will find ways to work together in cooperation to create harmony in the workplace and in their homes. That ultimately leads to harmony in our communities, cities, states, countries and in the world. It's time to tune out the biased news which focuses constantly on disharmony. The news only leads one to believe that the whole world is in a state of hell. This is not true. Soon, when more people demand it, there will be news programs that focus on all the wonderful things happening in the world—people helping each other, how love may have performed a miracle, companies that are cleaning up the environment, inventions for the future, special programs for refugees. There is so much good, and some of it is happening directly in the workplace.

There are some businesses beginning to recognize that production is greatly enhanced if employees are happy, and one of the ways to create happy employees is to give them greater say in business decisions, and greater flexibility in planning work schedules that really serve their needs. Many people are even working from home now. The really wise businesses are providing day-care centers to make it easier on employees who want to feel that their children are adequately provided for and may even want to visit them on their lunch hours. This greatly relieves the guilt many parents feel in having to leave their children all day to go to work. With so many people aging, it would be wonderful if businesses would also provide day-care for elders, so employees with elderly parents could better serve them.

All of us just want to be appreciated, and a boss who learns to show appreciation will have workers who want to please him or her. A person can take constructive criticism much more easily if there are words of appreciation prior to the criticism and following it, as well. Positive communication allows others to expand their self-esteem and confidence. There is no reason to communicate in any other way except for a person's own unresolved personal hang-ups. It's not necessary to project your problems onto others when you begin to gain self-awareness of your issues and take the responsibility to resolve them.

We even have the option of moving beyond the idea of needing a job, when we take total responsibility at all levels of our existence. Think back to relatively recent times when people lived off the land. Their "job" was living in harmony with nature in such a way that nature provided all they needed. The high stress industrialized lifestyle is what forces us into needing a job. Maybe it's time to move away from all that for those who can see the emptiness it offers.

"We are born and then we die" is a common phrase. What comes between those two realities of life is up to us. Let's choose to view our lives as wonderful opportunities to learn, and our work as service in some way to others. In this way we face death with a whole different perspective, feeling as though we lived a worthwhile existence, and feeling ready to move on to the last true adventure in life, dying. Death is only a rebirth into another dimensional reality as we drop away the body, the vehicle that served us while here in this world.

14

Death Is Not a Requirement

WE HAVE HEARD so many times that the only requirements in life are death and taxes. I am going to give you a different understanding. For one thing, there is a quiet revolution going on about taxes. More and more people are beginning to see the relationship between the Federal Reserve, which is not federal, and the IRS, which is different than we have been led to believe.

However, taxes and the government conspiracy issues are not the focus of this chapter or this book. Hopefully, I will leave you with enough curiosity to check this out on your own. Soon the masses will awaken to a completely different understanding about what is really going on in the world, and who is actually in charge. Some of our ET friends are assisting with that understanding, so more and more people will be better prepared for the great changes ahead. Again, I highly recommend the "Cosmic Disclosure" program on Gaia Television as the best way to learn about the changes and about the real history of our planet.

Death is not what we have believed it to be. First of all, it's an absolutely natural part of life on this planet, as is birth. It is definitely not the enemy, although we have a morbid fear of death in this culture, which is very sad. That fear has led our very backward medical institutions to treat the dying in less than humane ways, rather than allowing a person to die in peace with his or her loved ones present in a pleasant setting.

Many of the older generation may remember the movie, "Soylent Green." It wasn't a pleasant theme because ultimately human bodies were used as food made into green pellets. However, I will always remember one scene where a dying person was in a room where lovely music was playing with surround sound and video images of beautiful scenes in nature. How peaceful such a death would be, in contrast to invasive medical devices, doctors and nurses beating on your chest, and the cold, sterile atmosphere of a hospital.

Hospices have become commonplace in most cities, places where people can at least be given care and support while in the process of dying, but I believe there will be even more progress in the future. I believe we will have dying centers, just as we have birthing centers, and new traditions will arise around dying that will benefit all of us. Oregon was the first state to have a law allowing doctors to assist a person who was terminal and wanted to die with dignity. Other States may soon follow.

I spent six and a half weeks in India in the mid-80s. I visited Varanasi, sometimes known as "The City of Death." This is where many people go to die so their bodies may be cremated on the banks of the Ganges River. Most people in our culture think of this as being morbid, but I didn't see it that way at all. I saw the families coming together and being much more involved in the whole process of the death of their loved ones—making arrangements for wrapping the bodies which were carried through the streets to the banks of the river and placed on a funeral pyre. The ashes were given up to the river in what I felt was a positive ritual of death, but I must admit, I was glad women were no longer throwing themselves on the pyre of their husbands. I found all this much more spiritually satisfying than our Western approach to death; but then again, I felt a real kinship to India on many levels.

I remember once reading a book, possibly by Ram Dass, a wonderful American Swami. He was in this same city and apparently made a comment to an elderly gentleman, offering his condolences or at least expressing his sympathy in some manner. The gentleman responded by expressing that it was not he who was out of place. He was exactly where he chose to be, so he could die in a blessed location. It was he who felt sorry for this lone traveler who was truly out of place.

Every time I think about my experiences in that ancient city, which was previously known as Benares, I remember walking through the crowded, narrow streets of the oldest section of town with my companions. At one small, open area, we stopped for a moment, and an old gentleman sitting cross-legged on the ground reached up to me and handed me a beautiful flower. It was a water lily of the richest pink, a color in total contrast to the gray surroundings on this early, overcast morning. This is one of the special images that will stay with me forever, and I bless the old man in my mind whenever I remember him, as he blessed me by handing me the flower. I felt very honored.

Death is but a transition into another dimensional reality. A person's level of consciousness will determine what they experience as they cross over, but most will experience deceased loved ones welcoming them and assisting them to go toward the light, where they will experience a great sense of love and peace, beyond anything in this three-dimensional world. They will experience the divine presence of loving beings, depending on their religious orientation. They may be greeted by Christ or the Buddha or maybe the Native American Elders. Most in the western world will experience Jesus and possibly angelic beings.

There are many books on death or thanatology, which is the study of death. Dr. Elizabeth Kubler-Ross was an extraordinary pioneer in this field, as was Dr. Raymond Moody, who wrote one of the first books about near-death experiences in *Life After Life*. Almost all who have experienced NDE say they no longer fear death—that it is an exceptionally beautiful, peaceful process.

Another book by Dr. Moody, *Reunions*, compelled me to go to Anniston, Alabama, to study with him. We were a small group of therapists meeting in his lovely home right on Choccolocco Creek. It had at one time been Downings Mill, where wheat was ground into flour and corn was ground into meal. The mill had been remodeled into a three-story home filled with wonderful antiques, ancient artifacts, and playful cartoon art.

Dr. Moody taught us about the ancient Greek oracles of the dead and how people would go to underground caverns to meet apparitions of their deceased loved ones or historical leaders through elaborate rituals. Dr. Moody has recreated this technique for experiencing apparitions of deceased loved ones, and has embedded it in a therapeutic approach to grief counseling. We were there as therapists to learn this particular technique of grief counseling.

We have seen these new approaches to death and dying evolve over the last several decades, but what is now coming out in a very strong way is the idea of ascension. There are many books on ascension and at least one publisher, Oughten House Publications, specializes in this type of material. Conferences on ascension are springing up all over. Why is this idea suddenly taking flight in our culture, and what does it mean in the first place?

Ascension is the raising of the molecular vibration to the point where a person enters into a higher dimension while still in the body. Jesus did this as a visible demonstration of the power over death. It's an old book, but *The Celestine Prophecy* by James Redfield was very popular in the past, and it concluded with some of the key characters "disappearing" into light. That's what the whole "Ninth Insight" was all about in this interesting story. I am not talking about what some Christians call "rapture." Going into a higher dimension requires a higher level of consciousness to make the vibrational shift, not just thinking of yourself as a Christian. The most comprehensive book

I have seen on this topic is *The Ascension Mysteries* by David Wilcock.

The fact is that this planet is presently undergoing a dimensional, vibrational shift. There will be millions of people who will ascend during this time, but those will be the people who "awaken" to who they really are, a powerful, spiritual being of light. This is not about being "saved" in the way that some fundamentalist Christians believe. A pious belief structure is not a requirement for ascension. You need to do what Christ taught instead of expecting him to somehow do it for you just because on Sunday you happen to sit in a church pew. He taught love.

This whole book is really about ascension, because ascension is about love. How so, you might ask? It has to do with vibration or frequency. You must be able to shift your vibrational frequency upward and open your heart to love. Love is absolutely the most powerful force in the universe.

Many people know by now that in the East they talk of having seven primary chakras in the body. These are essentially energy focal points. Actually, there are more than seven, especially as we move into the dimensional shift, but for now we will focus on the original seven chakras, which are aligned with the endocrine system.

There are various approaches used in describing these chakras. The diagram on the opposite page shows one of the more basic configurations.

As you can see, the chakras are in a straight line from the base of the torso, following the spine, up to the top of the head. Each of them has an associated color, as well. Starting at the crown and working down, the colors are usually shown as violet, indigo, sky blue, green, yellow, or-

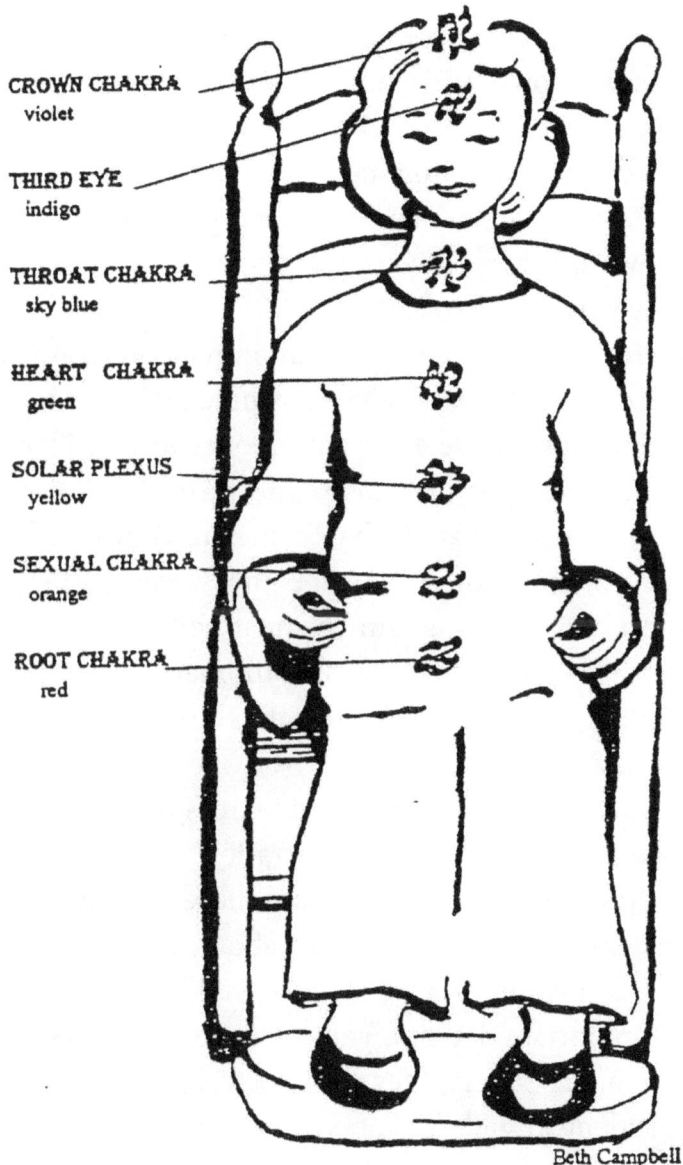

CHAKRA DIAGRAM

ange, and red at the base of the torso. Sometimes the colors vary slightly, but these are pretty standard. Amazon.com has numerous DVDs and books on chakras. There are some excellent guided chakra meditations, as well. Right now, all you need to focus on is opening your heart chakra, that is the green one. This opens you to love—love of self, love of others, love of peace, love of this planet, love of the whole universe.

The reason love is so important in relation to ascension is because it helps you raise your vibrational level. People who don't raise their vibrational level will not ascend, but will stay instead in the third-dimensional reality. Ultimately, that probably means death in the traditional sense. However, since the whole planet is presently experiencing a dimensional shift, those who aren't ready to make this shift will ultimately be reborn onto another planet that maintains the third-dimensional frequency.

As the frequency continues to increase on this planet, we will see even greater polarization into two basic groups, those who focus on fear and those who focus on love. That is what this book is all about, choosing love over fear. Is this important? Yes, yes, yes! It is absolutely the most important decision you can make right now, but it's not about just saying, "Yes, I think I'll choose love. That seems prudent to me." It is about making the choices in your life, the changes in your life that allow you to truly be in the love camp versus the fear camp.

This is where some of the government conspiracy proponents and some of the Christian fundamentalists, as well as Islamic fundamentalists or any other radical group, miss the boat. It is not about your belief system being right, it is about living love, peace, and harmony. Some of those who are aware that there is such a thing as a secret government come only from a fear base. They are only adding to the problem, just as the hellfire-and-damnation ministers are actually promoting fear, which is an absolute distortion, totally and completely, of what Jesus taught.

We have learned, hopefully, that what comes first is self-love. Self-love isn't being self-centered or selfish in the normal understanding of those words. Rather, it's self-respect and the awareness that you can't give away what you don't already have. Perception also plays an important role in death. If a person doesn't make some sort of effort toward spiritual growth in his or her lifetime, that person will have a different perceptual experience at death than someone who is spiritually evolved. Everything we do here while in physical form is about spiritual growth, whether a person understands it that way or not. How much better it is to awaken fully now. There is so much to learn here, so many obstacles we can learn to overcome if we put our collective minds to it.

I cannot say for certain that all I have revealed in this book will happen exactly as I have described. I can only say that it represents my best sense of things at this moment. I, too, am on my own spiritual path toward self-awareness and enlightenment. There are many evolved beings who view ascension a little differently, each one with his or her own interpretation. There have also been numerous prophesies with specific dates, but time, as we perceive it, is only relevant in this dimension. Also, human consciousness is constantly affecting what happens in this world.

I choose to experience life almost as an anthropologist—observing, but not judging. I just say internally, "That's very interesting," as I encounter various viewpoints. I hope you can read this book with a similar frame of mind: being open and non-judgmental, allowing it to speak to you at a deeper more profound level where your own intuitive resources can determine what is right for you.

Above all else, recognize that this is truly a time of choices and important decisions. You can move more into the light or recede into darkness. The choice is yours to make. I only hope that you decide to choose love. It is up to you to choose your own destiny. I feel grateful because I know deep within me that millions of people will make just that choice, and it will change the world as we know it. It will be like millions of butterflies breaking through into the light at the same, precise moment. It will be awesome in the truest sense of that word, and we will be right there in the midst of it.

Resources

A Course in Miracles, Combined Volume. Foundation for Inner Peace, Mill Valley, CA, 2007.

Alexander, Eben. *Proof of Heaven: A Neurosurgeon's Journey Into the Afterlife.* Simon & Schuster, NY, 2012.

Baba Ram Dass. *Be Love Now: The Path of the Heart.* Harper Collins, NY, 2010.

Baba Ram Dass. *Remember: Be There Now.* (Transformation of Richard Alpert, Ph.D, Harvard Psychologist). Lama Foundation, San Cristobal, New Mexico, 1978.

Bass, Ellen and Laura Davis. *The Courage to Heal: A Guide for Woman Survivors of Child Sexual Abuse.* Harper Collins, NY, 2008.

Berzon Ph.D, Betty. *The Intimacy Dance: A Guide to Long-Term Success in Gay and Lesbian Relationships.* Penguin Putnam Books, NY, 1996.

Berzon Ph.D, Betty. *Permanent Partners: Building Gay and Lesbian Relationships that Last.* Penguin Group, 2004.

Brandon, Nathaniel. *The Six Pillars of Self-Esteem*. A Bantam Book, NY, 1994.

Canfield, Jack and Jacqueline Miller. *Heart at Work: Stories and Strategies for Building Self-Esteem and Reawakening the Soul at Work*. McGraw Hill, NY, 1996.

Carey, Ken. Vision: *A Personal Call to Create a New World*. Harper Collins, NY, 1992.

Carey, Ken. *The Starseed Transmissions*. Harper Collins, NY, 1982.

Chodron, Pema. *When Things Fall Apart: Heart Advice for Difficult Times*. Shambala Hall, Boston, MA, 1997.

Chopra MD, Deepak. *Quantum Healing: Exploring the Frontiers of Mind/Body Medicine*. Bantam Books, NY, 1989.

Daily Word. Unity, 1901 NW Blue Parkway, Unity Village, MO 64065-0001.

Dean, Robert O. *Secrets from the Underground Vol 6 Coverup & Hybrids* (DVD). Amazon.com, manufactured on demand, 2007.

Dyer, Dr Wayne W. *I Can See Clearly Now*. Hay House, NY, 2014.

Eker, T. Harv. *Secrets of the Millionaire Mind: Think Rich to Get Rich*. Harper Collins, NY, 2005.

Faber, Adele and Elaine Mazlish. *How to Talk so Kids Will Listen & Listen so Kids Will Talk*. Avon Books, NY, 1999.

Fiore Ph.D., Edith. *Encounters: A Psychologist Reveals Case Studies of Abductions by Extratrerrestrials.* Doubleday, NY, 1989.

Friedlander, Shems. *Rumi and the Whirling Dervishes.* Parabola Books, NY, 2003.

Gawain, Shakti. *Creative Visualization: Use the Power of Your Imagination to Create What You Want in Your Life.* (25th Anniversary Edition). Nataraj Publishing, Novato, CA, 2002.

Golden Star Alliance. *I'm OK I'm Just Mutating.* Golden Star Publishing, Hawaii, 2007.

Gosman, Fred G. *Spoiled Rotten: Today's Children and How to Change Them.* Warner Books, NY, 1990.

Grattan, Brian. *Mahatma I & II: The I Am Presence.* Light Technology Publishing, Flafstaff, AZ, 1994.

Greer MD, Steven M. *Contact: Countdown to Transformation.* Crossing Point Inc., Crozet, VA, 2009.

Haines Ph.D., Richard F. *CE-5: Close Encounters of the Fifth Kind.* Sourcebooks Inc., Naperville, IL, 1999.

Haraldson Ph.D., Erlendur. *Modern Miracles: The Story of Sathya Sai Baba: A Modern Day Prophet.* White Crow Books, UK, 1987.

Harrison, Lewis. *Spiritual Not Religious: Sacred Tools for Modern Times.* Ask Lewis Publishers, Stamford , NY, 2014.

Hay, Louise. You Can Heal Your Life. (Gift Edition). Hay House, NY, 1999.

Hebb, Michael. "Death Over Dinner." Ted Med Talk, 2013, deathoverdinner.org.

Jampolsky MD, Gerald G. *Love Is Letting Go of Fear.* Bantam Books, NY, 1981.

Jarow, Rick. *Creating the Work You Love: Courage, Commitment, and Career.* Destiny Books, VT, 1995.

Jones Ph.D., C. B. Scott and Angela T. Smith Ph.D. *Voices from the Cosmos.* Headline Books Inc., Terra Alta, WV, 2014.

Kelly Ph.D., Joseph F. *The Ecumenical Councils of the Catholic Church: A History.* Liturgical Press, Collegeville, MN, 2009.

Langley, Noel and Cayce, Hugh Lynn, ed. *Edgar Cayce on Reincarnation.* 1967.

Lapseritis MS, Kewaunee. *The Sasquatch People and Their Interdimensional Connection.* Comanche Spirit Publishing, Seattle, WA, 2011.

Lawlor, Robert. *Sacred Geometry: Philosophy & Practice.* Thames & Hudson, London, 1982.

Leith, John B. *Genesis for the Space Race: The Inner Earth and the Extraterrestrials.* Time Stream Pictures and Books, Ooltewahm, TN, 2014.

Luskin, Dr Fred. *Forgive for Good: A Proven Prescription for Health and Happiness.* Harper One, NY, 2002.

Mack MD, John E. *Abductions: Human Encounters With Aliens.* Scribner, NY, 1994.

Mara, Jill. *Keys to Soul Evolution: A Gateway to the Next Dimension*. 7D Publishing, St. Thomas, USVI, 2009.

Marler, David. Triangular *UFOs: An Estimate of the Situation*. Richard Delan Press, Rochester, NY, 2013.

Martin, Joel and Patricia Romanowski. *We Don't Die: George Anderson's Conversations With the Other Side*. The Berkley Publishing Group, NY, 2002.

Melchizedek, Drunvalo. T*he Ancient Secret of the Flower of Life, Vol. I* (1999), *Vol. II* (2000). Light Technology Publishing, Flagstaff, AZ.

Miller, Ronald S. and *The Editors of New Age Journal. As Above, So Below: Paths to Spiritual Renewal in Daily Life*. Tarcher Publishing, 1992.

Millman, Dan. *The Life You Were Born to Live: A Guide to Finding Your Life Purpose*. New World Library, NY, 1993.

Moody, Jr. MD, Raymond. *Life After Life: The Best-selling Original Investigation that Reveals "Near-Death Experiences."* Harper Collins, NY, 2015.

Moody MD, Raymond with Paul Perry. *Reunions: Visionary Encounters With Departed Loved Ones*. Ballantine Books, NY, 1994.

Moody MD, Raymond with Paul Perry. *Paranormal: My Life in Pursuit of the Afterlife*. Harper Collins, NY, 2012.

Murphet, H. Sai Baba: *Man of Miracles*. Samuel Weiser Inc., York Beach, ME, 1971.

Noel, Brook and Pamela D. Blair Ph.D. *I Wasn't Ready to Say Good-bye: Surviving, Coping and Healing After the Sudden Death of a Loved One*. Champion Press Ltd., Milwaukee, WI, 2000.

Pollard III, John K. *Self-Parenting: The Complete Guide to Your Inner Conversations*. Generic Human Studies Publishing, Malibu, CA, 1987.

Ray, Sondra. *The Loving Relationships Treasury*. Celestial Arts, Berkeley, CA, 2006.

Redfield, James. *The Celestine Prophecy: An Adventure*. Grand Central Publishing, NY, 1993.

Redfield, James. *The Tenth Insight: Holding the Vision*. Warner Books, NY, 1996.

Romanek, Lisa. *From My Side of the Bed: Pulling Back the Covers on Extraterrestrial Contact. A Spouse's Point of View*. Etherean LLC, Colorado, 2011.

Romanek, Stan with J. Allan Danelek. *Messages: The World's Most Documented Extraterrestrial Contact Story*. Llewellyn Publications, Woodbury. MN, 2009.

Royal, Lyssa and Keith Priest. *Preparing for Contact: A Metamorphosis of Consciousness*. Royal Priest Research Press, Phoenix, AZ, 1993.

Russell, Peter. *From Science to God: A Physicist's Journey Into the Mystery of Consciousness*. New World Library, Novato, CA, 2002.

Salla Ph.D., Michael E. *Galactic Diplomacy: Getting to Yes With ET*. Exopolitics Institute, Kealakekua, HI, 2013.

Salla Ph.D., Michael E. *Insiders Reveal Secret Space Programs & Exterrestrial Alliances*. Exopolitics Institute, Pakoa, HI, 2015.

Sears, Jerry. *A Course In Miracles in 5 Minutes*. Associates Publishers, 1994.

Sprinkle, Dr R. Leo. *Soul Samples: Personal Explorations in Reincarnation and UFO Experiences*. Granite Publishing LLC, Colombus, NC, 1999.

Steiger, Brad with Sherry Hanson Steiger. *Angels On Their Shoulders*. Ballantine Books, 1994.

Stone Ph.D., Joshua David. *Beyond Ascension: How to Complete the Seven Levels of Initiation*. Light Technology, Flagstaff, AZ, 1995.

Stone Ph.D., Joshua David. *Soul Psychology: How to Clear Negative Emotions and Spiritualize Your Life*. Ballantine Wellspring, The Random House Publishing Group, 1999.

Stone Ph.D., Joshua David. *The Complete Ascension Manual: How to Achieve Ascension in this Lifetime*. Light Technology Publishing, Flagstaff, AZ, 1994.

Strieber, Whitney. *The Key: A True Encounter*. Jeremy P. Tarcher/Penguin, NY, 2011.

Strieber, Whitney. *Communion: A True Story*. Avon Books, NY, 1988.

Sun Bear and Wabun Wind. *Black Dawn, Bright Day: Indian Prophecies for the Millennium That Reveal the Fate of the Earth*. Simon & Schuster, NY, 1992.

The Urantia Book. Uversa Press, NY, 2003.

Vaughn-Lee, Llewellyn (ed.) and Sara Sviri (biographical notes). *Traveling the Path of Love: Sayings of Sufi Masters.* The Golden Sufi Center, Inverness, CA, 1995.

Wanderer, Dr Zev and Tracy Cabot, Ph.D. *Letting Go: A 12-Week Personal Action Program to Overcome a Broken Heart.* Dell Publishing, NY, 1978.

Watkins, Leslie and Christopher Miles. *Alternative 003.* Avon Books, NY, 1977.

Weiss MD, Brian L. and Amy F. Weiss. *Miracles Happen: The Transformational Healing Power of Past-Life Memories.* Harper Collins, NY, 2013.

Wilber, Ken. *A Brief History of Everything.* Shambala Publications, Boston, MA, 1996.

Wilcock, David and Corey Goode, "Cosmic Disclosure." Television Series, Gaia TV, 2015.

Wilcock, David. *The Synchronicity Key: The Hidden Intelligence Guiding the Universe and You.* Plume, Reprint Edition, 2014.

Wilcock, David. *The Ascension Mysteries: Revealing the Cosmic Battle Between Good and Evil.* Dutton, NY, 2016

Williamson, Marianne. *A Return to Love: Reflections on the Principles of A Course in Miracles.* Harper Collins, NY, 1992.

Williamson, Marianne. *The Gift of Change: Spiritual Guidance for a Radically New Life.* Harper San Francisco, NY, 2004.

Winn, Marie. *The Plug-In Drug: Television, Computers, and Family Life: The Landmark Book About How Children Get Hooked on TV*. Penguin Group, NY, 2002.

Woolger Ph.D., Roger J. *Other Lives, Other Selves: A Jungian Psychotherapist Discovers Past-Lives*. Doubleday, NY, 1987.

Yogananda, Paramahansa. *Metaphysical Meditations*. Self Realization Fellowship, Los Angeles, CA, 1994.

Yogananda, Paramahansa. *Autobiography of a Yogi*. Start Publishing LLC, 2012.

About the Author

Dr. Barbie J. Taylor was known more affectionately as "Dr. Barbie" to her friends and clients. She graduated from the University of Washington in 1978 with a Ph.D. in clinical psychology, then began the first phase of her career as the Research Coordinator at the Center for Marital and Sexual Studies in Long Beach, California, where she also began her private practice as a clinical psychologist.

Preferring to be "on the move," ultimately she taught two hundred psychology students Human Sexual Behavior at Arizona State University, and an extension class at the University of West Virginia on Contemporary Issues in Parapsychology.

She was in private practice in California, Arizona, West Virginia, Pennsylvania, and Nevada. While in the east, Dr. Barbie became a regular on television and radio as well. She continued doing radio as one of the "Romance Doctors" in Irvine, California.

Dr. Barbie moved to Nevada in 1992, while employed as a private consultant for the Bigelow Foundation, which was funding parapsychological research. Her job was to find the world's greatest psychic medium. She chose George Anderson, and referred Mr. Bigelow to him. Mr. Bigelow ultimately funded some of George Anderson's research.

She also did research during the 90s with CSETI (Center for the Study of Extraterrestrial Intelligence), with Dr. Steven Greer. She retired as a psychologist in 2014 after more than thirty years in practice, and moved to Pahrump, Nevada, where she enjoyed her remaining years writing full-time.

Dr. Barbie made her transition on August 21, 2017.

www.ingramcontent.com/pod-product-compliance
Lightning Source LLC
Chambersburg PA
CBHW051654040426
42446CB00009B/1125